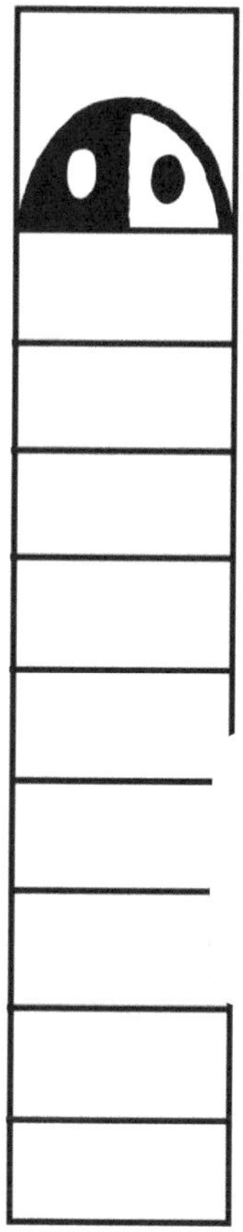

The Patchwork House of Night

UJWAL MANTHA

Welcome to the House!

What if all the years of your life were condensed into a physical place you could travel through? What if all those emotions, feelings and adventures were turned into a building that you could scale?

The Patchwork House of Night is my attempt to answer the question with the 23 years of my own life. The House came into being one canvas every day over the month of October with each floor touching on different themes ranging from freedom, nostalgia and hope to loss and responsibility.

Each canvas is accompanied by a journal entry that offers a snippet into my mind as I travel through what I've imagined as the summation of my entire life. The Patchwork House of Night deals with a variety of themes but fundamentally it is about transformation. It is about how everything changes, and each situation calls on different parts of oneself to address it. The Patchwork House of Night is a celebration of change. It is a tribute to how far I've come and how much I've changed.

The work was made entirely over the month of October 2022, as a part of Inktober, with one canvas being made every day. Each piece is steeped in lore and context, inviting the audience to go deeper and truly engage with the work.

Whilst the subject matter is undoubtedly intimate, it is my dearest hope that viewers find the feelings and symbols discussed in this work to be relatable and accessible.

This project exists in the space between two simple statements:

"I'M OLDER THAN I'VE EVER BEEN"

&

"I'M YOUNGER THAN I'LL EVER BE".

- Ujwal Mantha

Content

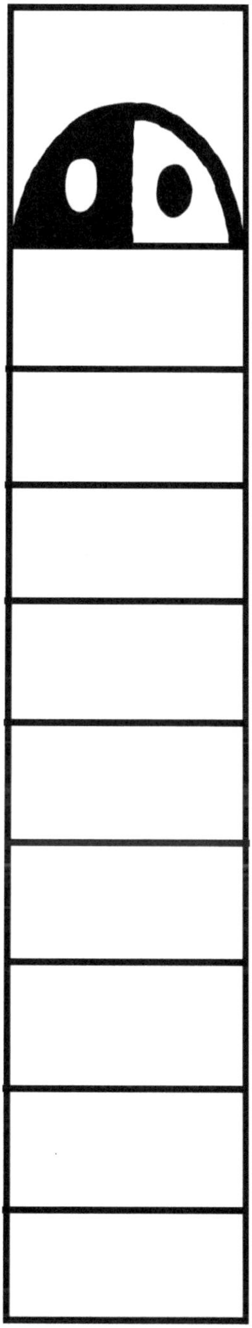

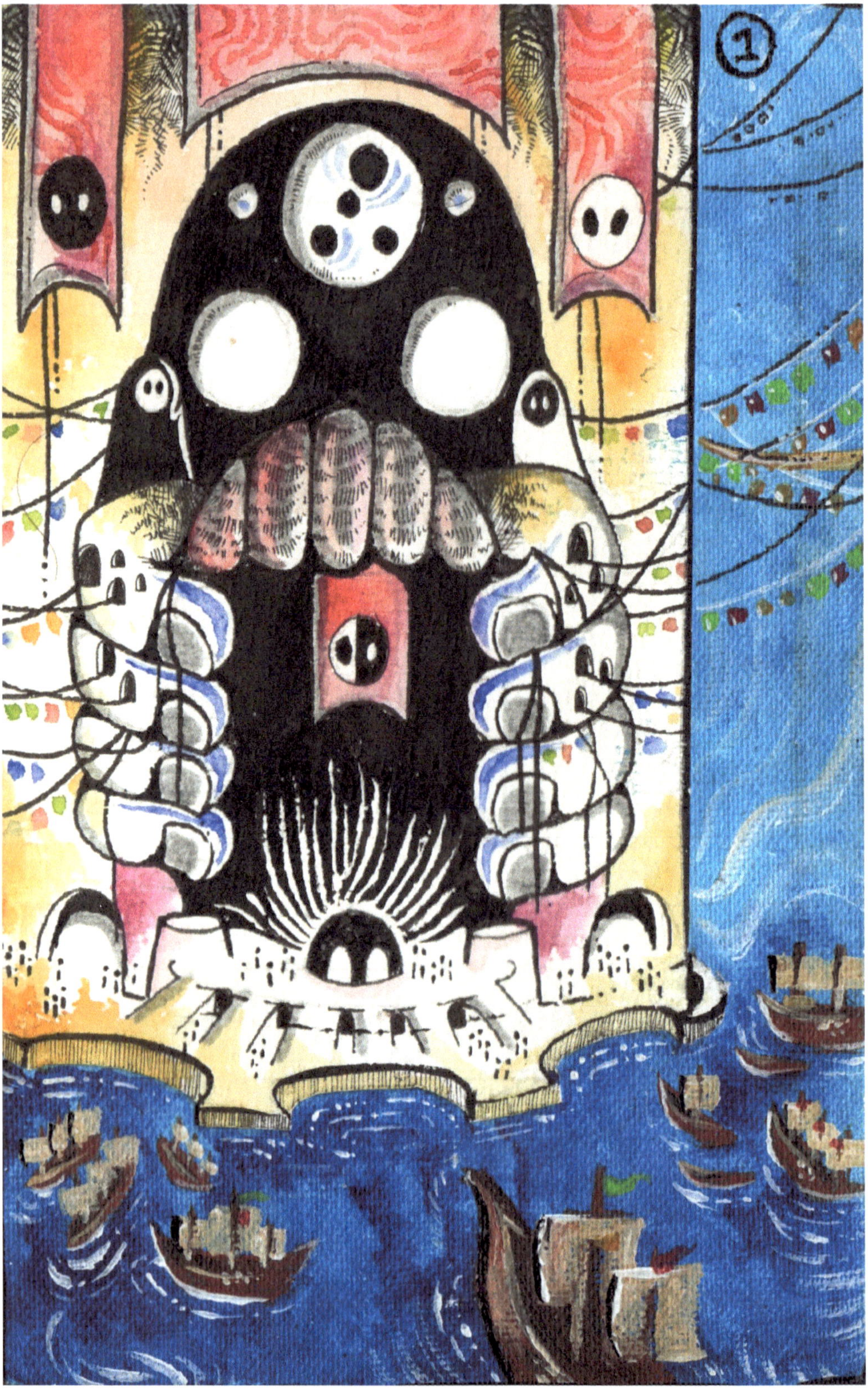
1

The Harbour

OCT 0 1 2022

I'm older than I've ever been
You'd think...
After millennia, we'd have figured out
how to talk about growing up.
Wasn't I just 12 last week?
I swear I was 17 yesterday?
What happened?

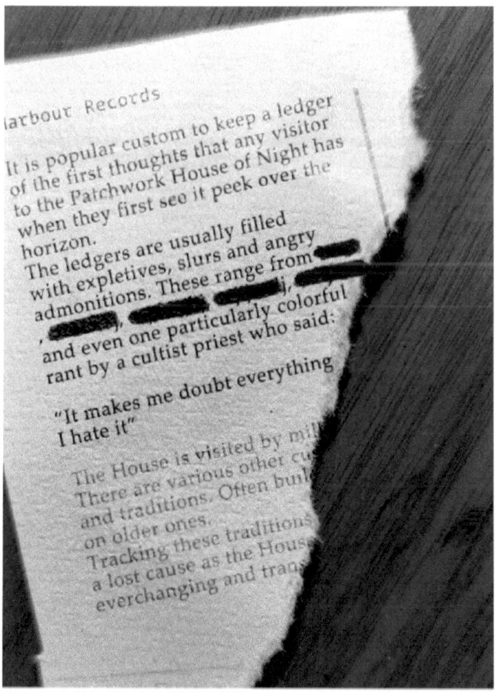

Over the next month, I'm going to be exploring the Patchwork House of Night.
This is a rite of passage for me and I do hope it will be enjoyable to you

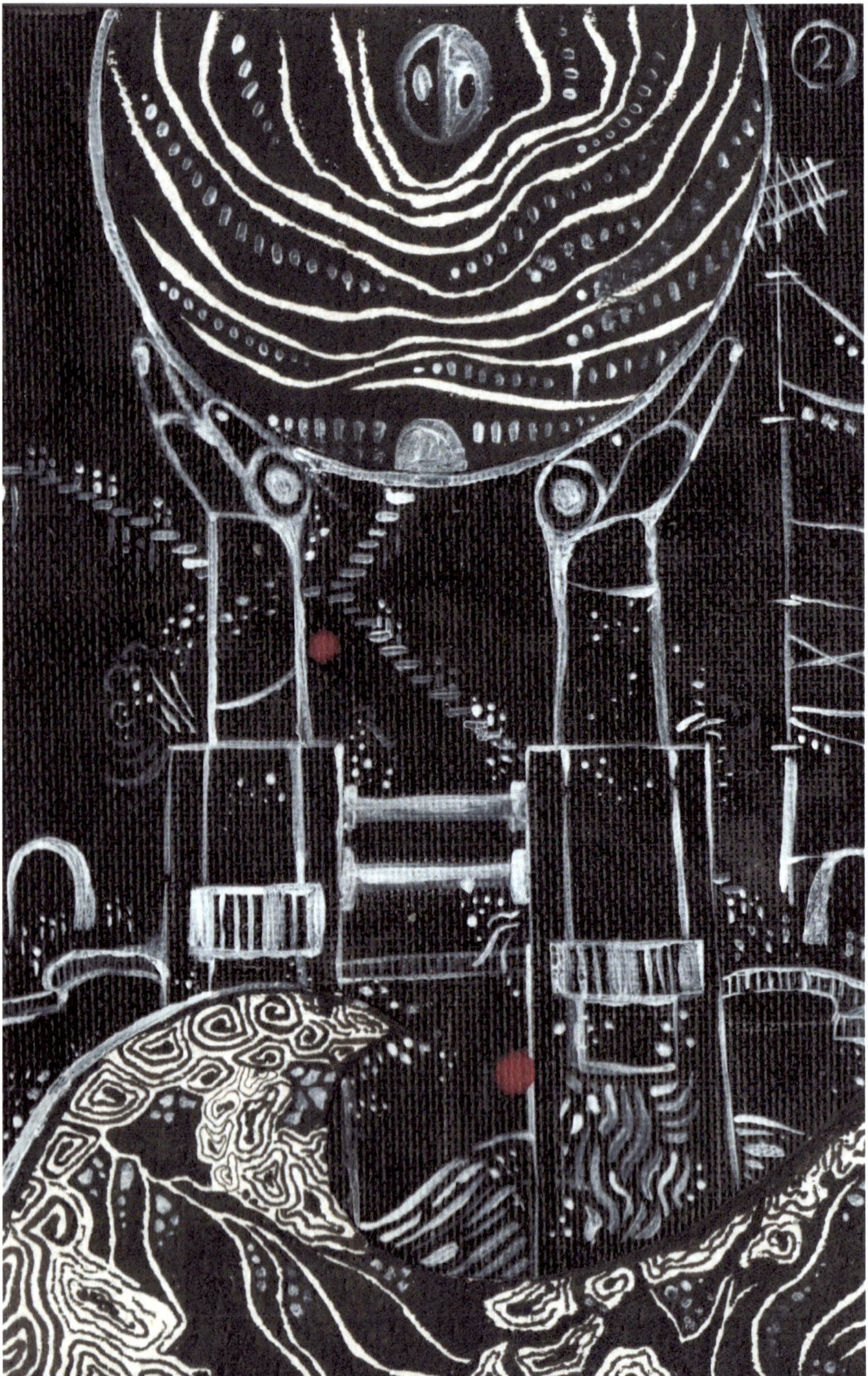

The Elevator

OCT 02 2022

The elevator, depending on the day and time, skips ahead to the good or bad parts of being me.

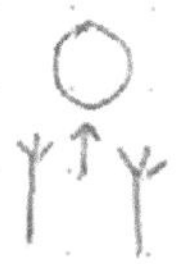

Those hands are pistons. You're literally thrown up.

We're taking the stairs though.
I want to know every part, every floor of the 23 year old, timeless Patchwork house of Night

I'm often inclined to skip over parts of myself, take the elevator past aspects of me that I have forgotten or simply don't wish to look directly at.

Now, we're going to take the stairs.

I'm going to look at every part of myself closely.

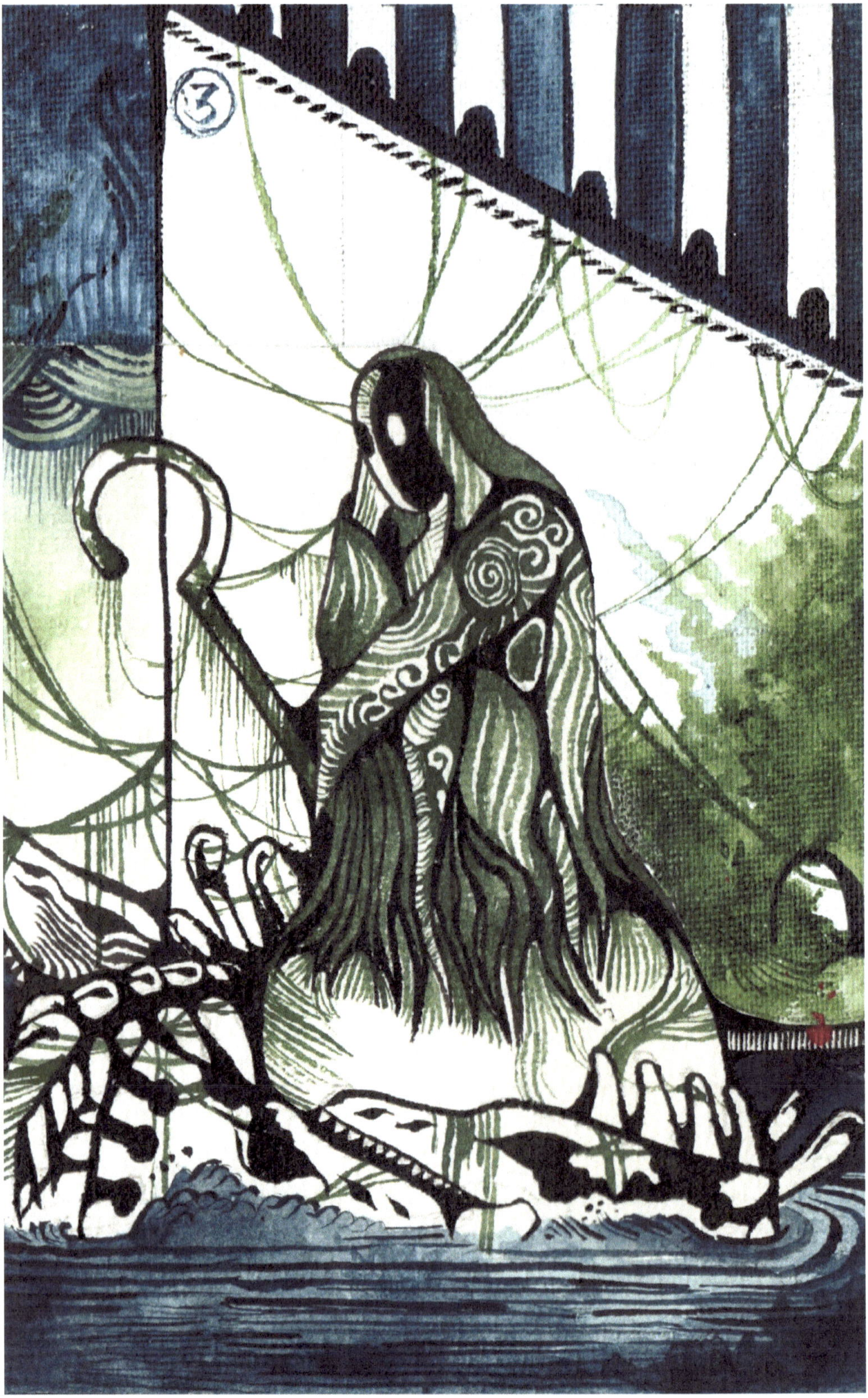
3

The Ruins

OCT 03 2022

Nobody comes here, to the ruins. They usually get on the elevator long before.
I'm alone here but for a few archeologists.
The Patchwork house grows every year.
It is a living thing and in it's form are the remnants of the things it used to be

It is said that this statue is the living body of the Patchwork Shepherd and that they are still alive to this day. They were tasked to watch over Ebb and Flo, the Cerebral Dragons, many aeons ago.
They have not moved in as many years.
and the skeletons of Ebb and Flo lie overgrown at their feet.
Under them lies countless other trinkets, remnants and memories
of the House's past.
Everyday there are countless archeologists and researchers chipping away at the ground and clearing the vines...
but there are some things they will never unbury.

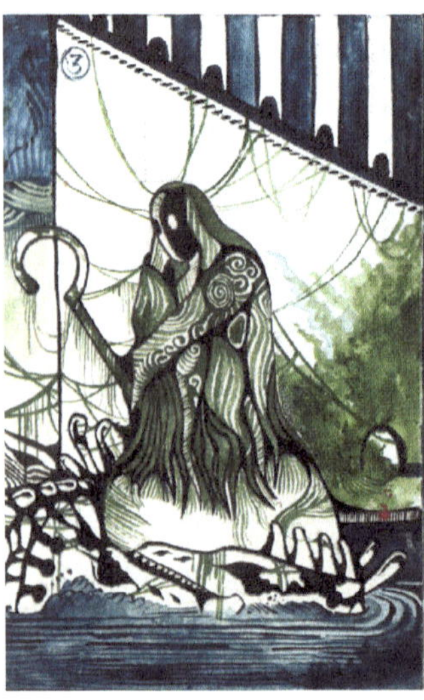

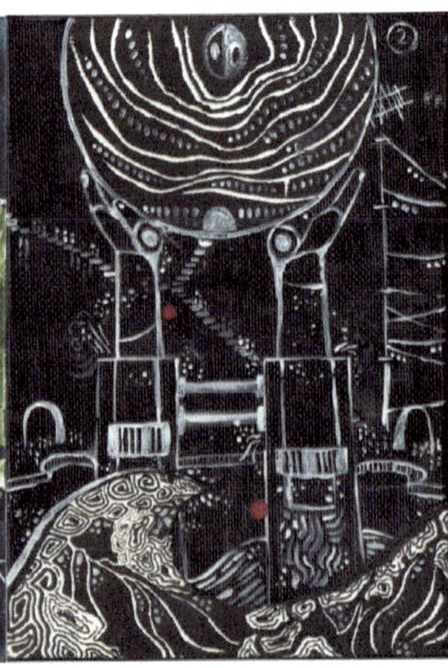

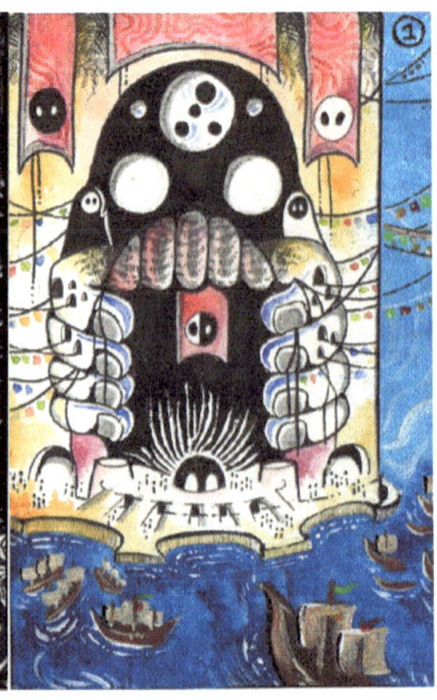

AGE

I'm every age
I have ever been
All time ever does
is pass and all I ever do is remember

-sue zhao

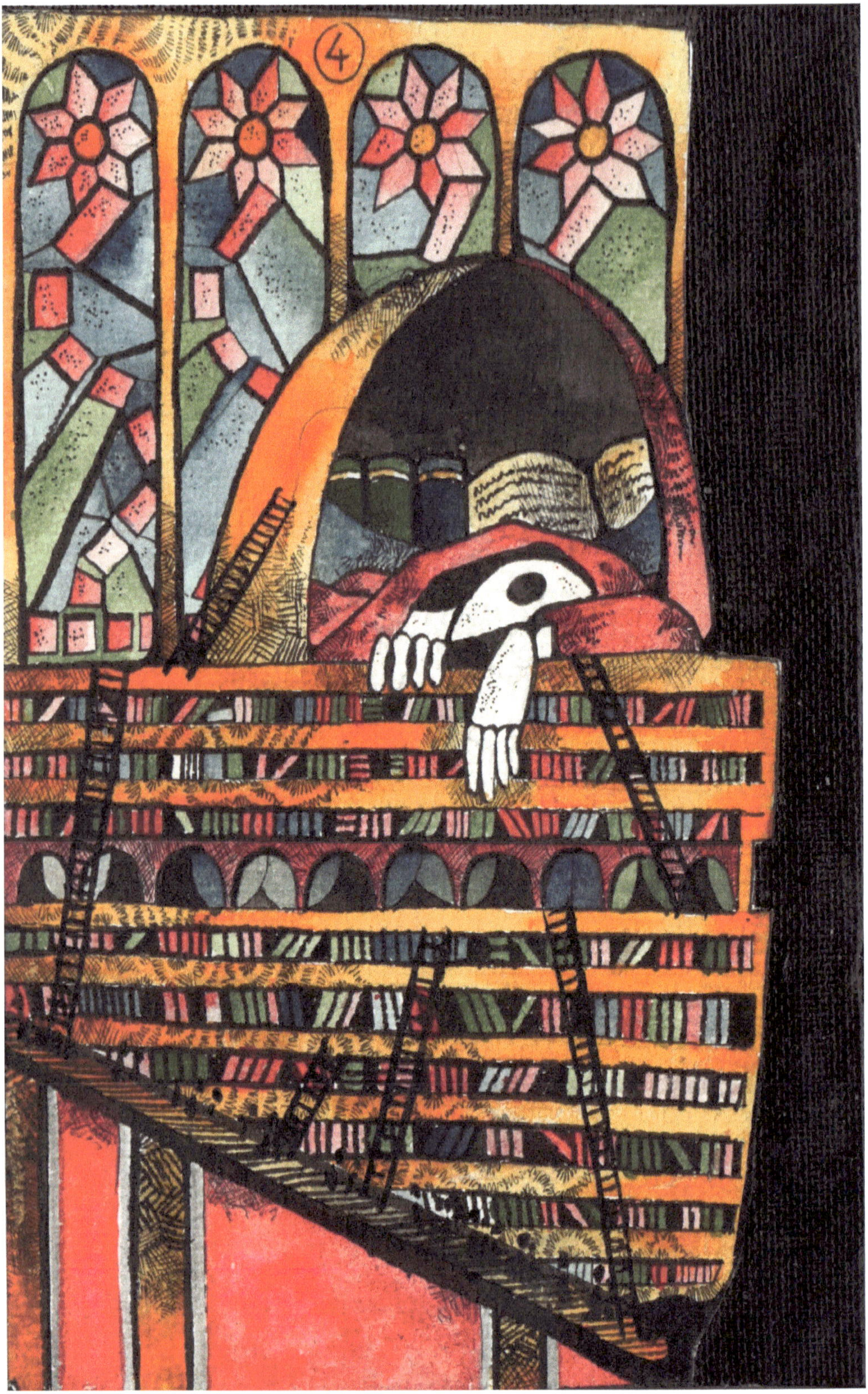
4

The Library

OCT 04 2022

With it's endless collections, beautiful design and lax return policy,
the Patchwork library is enchanting.
Every thing I've ever done
Every person I've ever met
Every person I've ever been
is stored here. What am I? But a series of stories
that bleed into each other.
But the librarian is asleep and hasn't been awake forever
So everytime I remember, a little bit gets lost
and I have to fill in the gaps of what is left behind.

Aren't we all just the stories we tell about ourselves? The Patchwork Library is a frequent stop for any visitor to the House. The Librarian is asleep (or a statue, it is unclear). People walk in. They take what they'd like.
But this is unfair of me to be bitter about. A little bit of me does get lost whenever I check out a book and maybe don't return it in the same condition. But for every thought I take (or forget), there is another I give.
People add to the library. It is made of books and stories and those are written (and rewritten) everyday.

We are all curious collages, weird little planetoids that grow by accreting other people's habits and ideas and styles and tics and jokes and phrases and tunes and hopes and fears as if they were meteorites that came soaring out of the blue, collided with us, and stuck. What at first is an artificial, alien mannerism slowly fuses into the stuff of our self, like wax melting in the sun, and gradually becomes as much a part of us as it was of someone else (though that person may very well have borrowed it from someone else to begin with)

From I Am a Strange Loop by Douglas Hofstadter

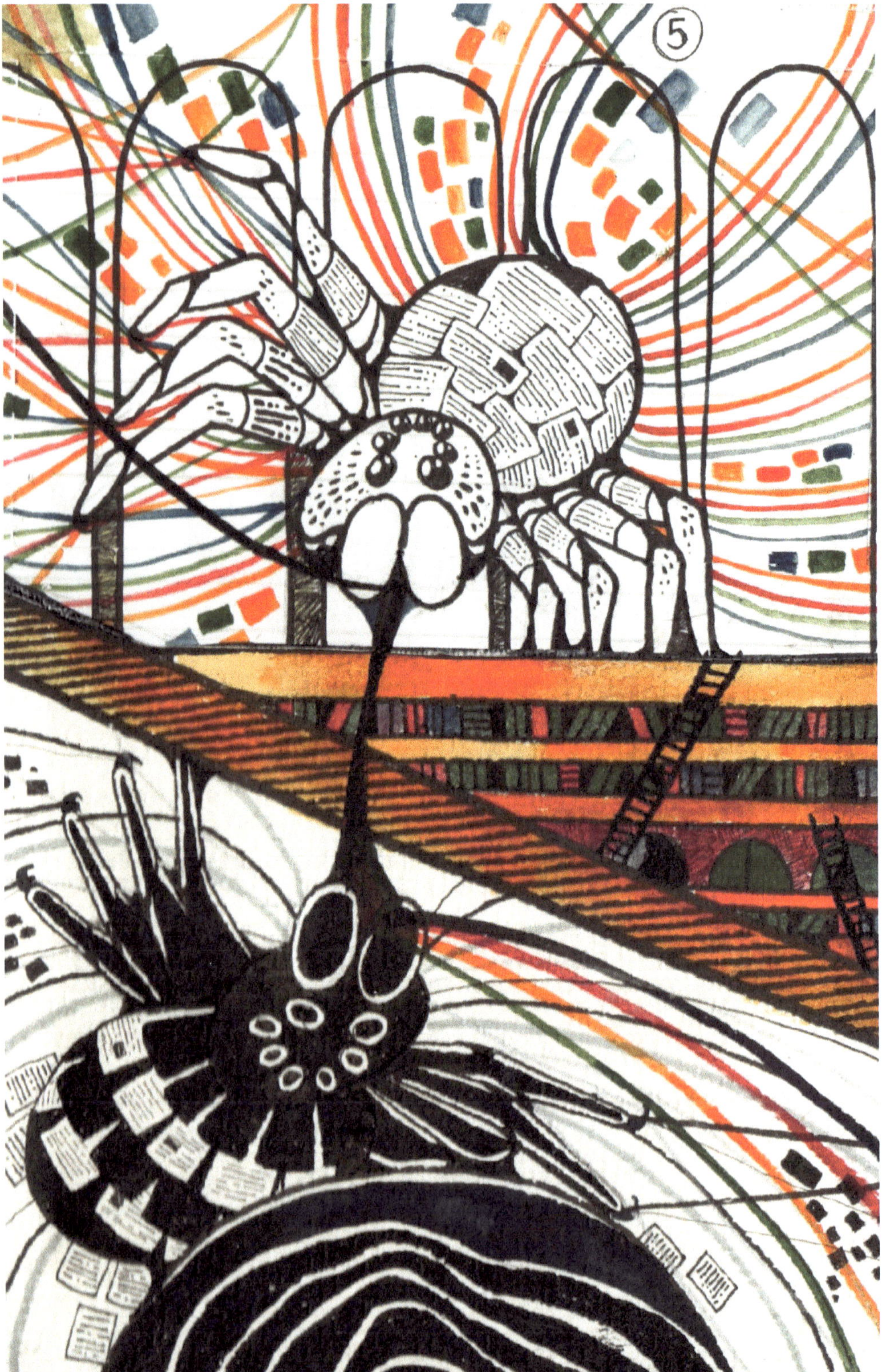
5

The Archives

OCT 05 2022

The Patchwork Spiders.

Gurthu & MatiMarapu

One weaves, the other unravels
One binds, the other frees
One remembers and the other forgets
I can't believe in destiny
I can't believe in some master plan
How can I? when I've seen first-hand that
everything that is written can be rewritten.

As you walk up the stairs you'll find the Patchwork spiders hard at work. They supply the library with all its books. Gurthu knits memories together and then Matimarapu unravels them.

In this dance, all time passes through the Patchwork House of Night.

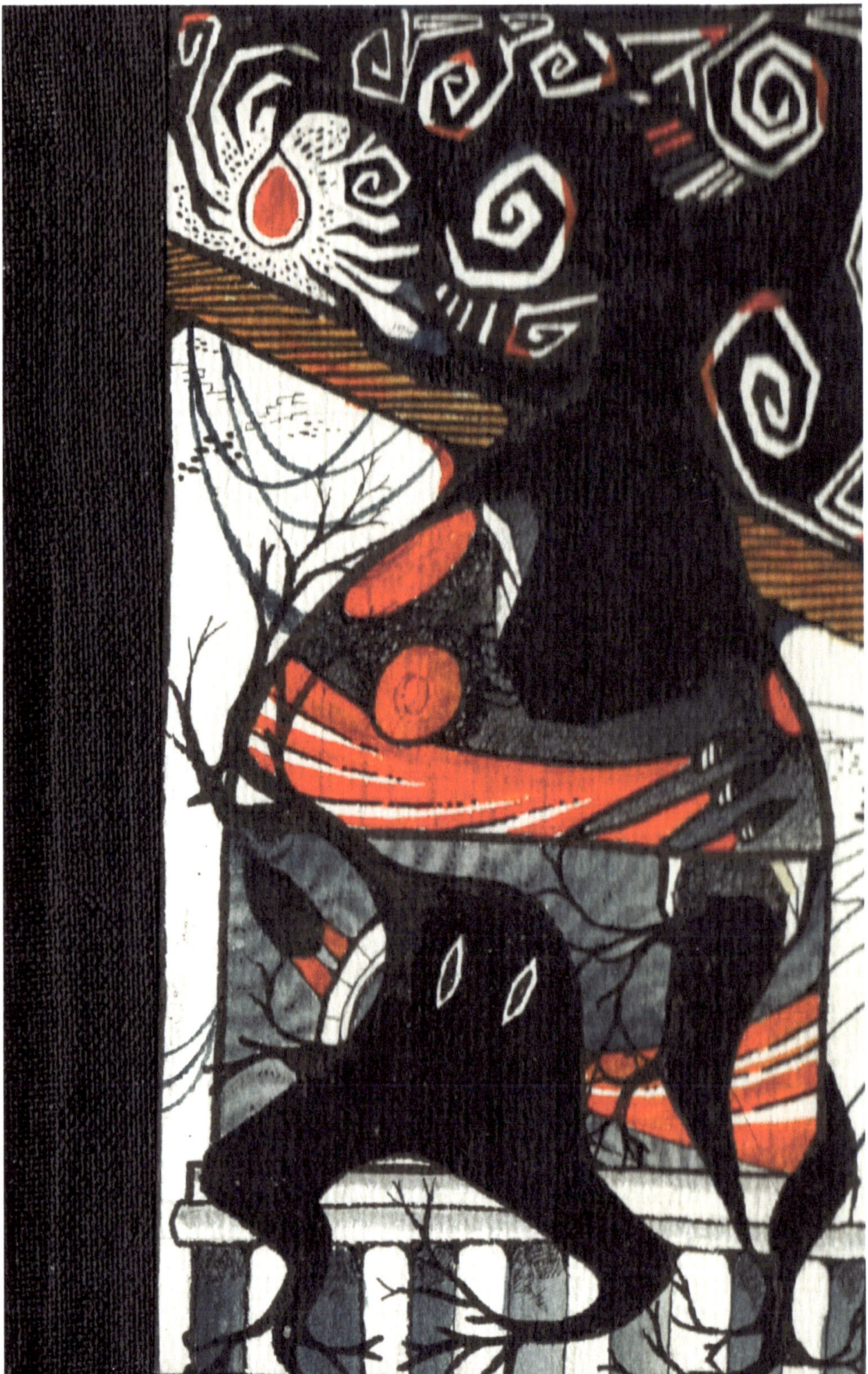

The Old Outpost

OCT 0 6 2022

I found an old outpost
Overgrown, forgotten
It's walls covered in rich mosaics. Dreams of a life that never
came to be. Dreams of stars and spacewalks
Two roads diverged in a yellow wood
I took one and let the other grow over
but I never forgot it.

From third grade to the first year of university I wanted to be an astronaut. I got into University for Astrophysics. For the longest time, I saw a future in the stars. I saw myself traveling to them and leaving a legacy on what is truly mankind's greatest frontier.

I also hated calculus and how boring the classes got. It took a few semesters of that for me to understand that what drew me to the stars were the grander, poetic feelings they inspired and not the pursuit of them.

I moved over into the arts where I could now pursue those grand feelings everyday. I chose a different path but I had dedicated so much of myself to the sciences that they left a permanent mark on the House of Night. Covering the towering House are monuments, old outposts, and forgotten archives dedicated to a dream long buried.

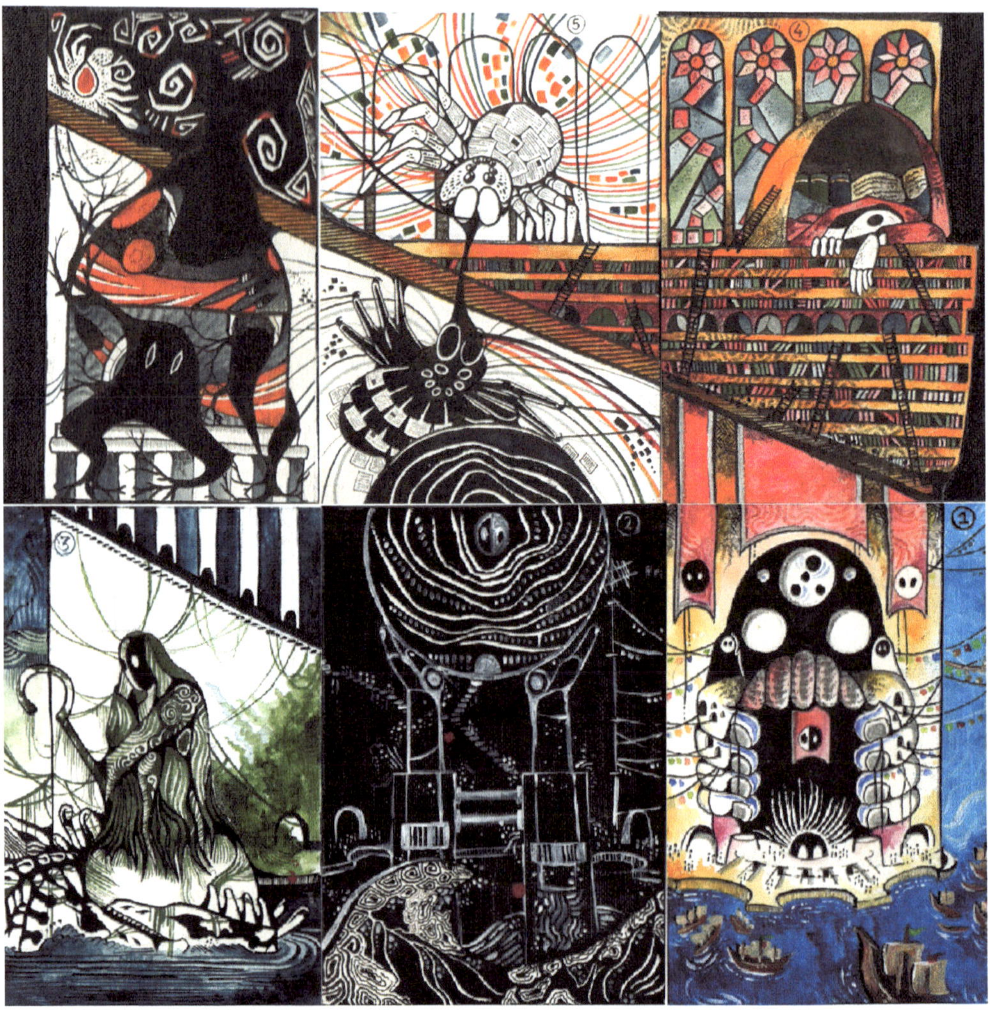
5
4
3
2
1

CHOICE

"I saw my life branching out before me like the green fig tree in the story. From the tip of every branch, like a fat purple fig, a wonderful future beckoned and winked.

One fig was a husband and a happy home and children, and another fig was a famous poet and another fig was a brilliant professor, and another fig was Ee Gee, the amazing editor, and another fig was Europe and Africa and South America, and another fig was Constantin and Socrates and Attila and a pack of other lovers with queer names and offbeat professions, and another fig was an Olympic lady crew champion, and beyond and above these figs were many more figs I couldn't quite make out.

I saw myself sitting in the crotch of this fig tree, starving to death, just because I couldn't make up my mind which of the figs I would choose. I wanted each and every one of them, but choosing one meant losing all the rest, and, as I sat there, unable to decide, the figs began to wrinkle and go black, and, one by one, they plopped to the ground at my feet."

Sylvia Plath, The Bell Jar

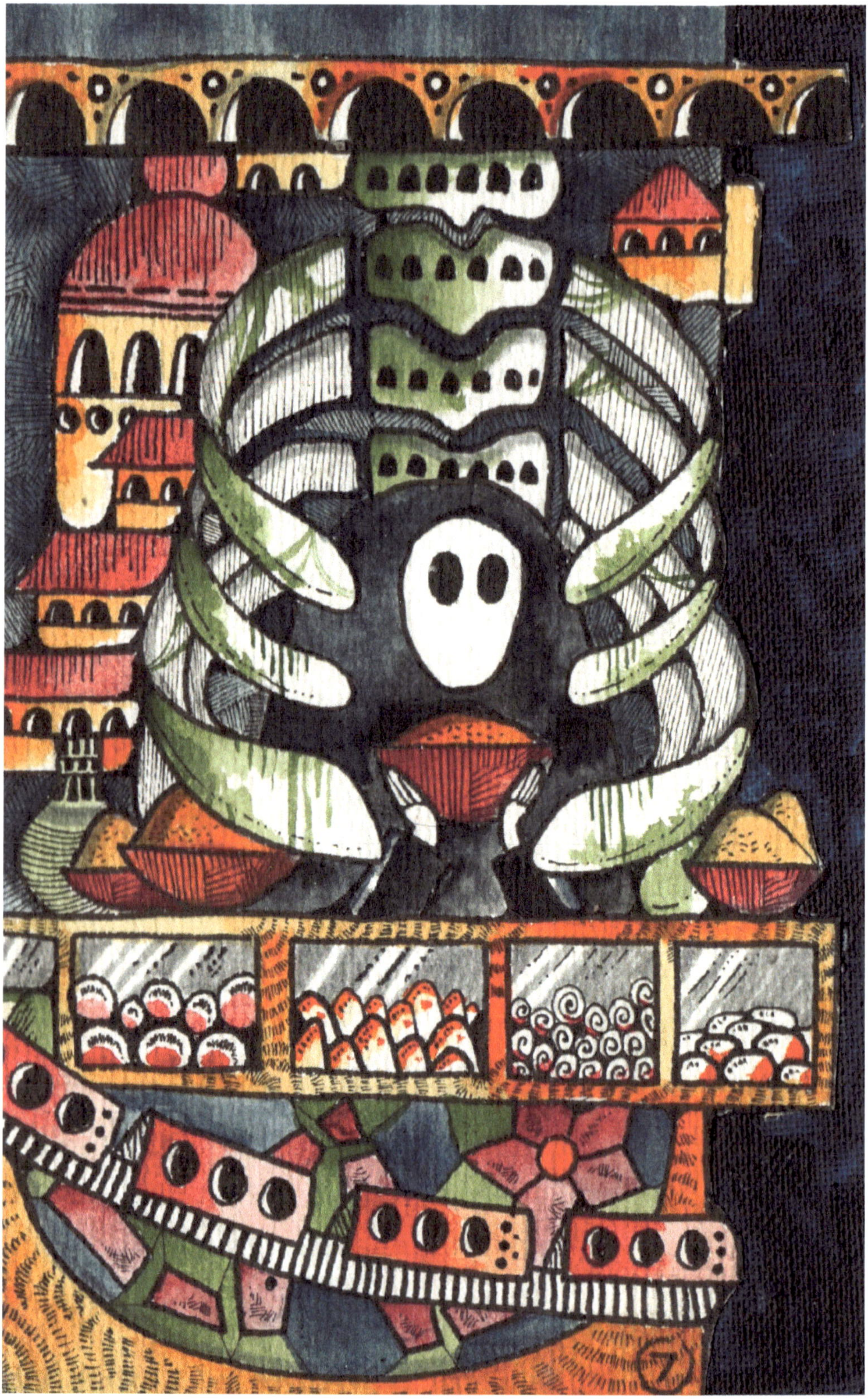

The Bazaar

OCT 07 2022

Every day people flock to the Bazaar.
You can buy anything there. Ideas, Interests, earworms ..etc.
Everyday the vendor lovingly packs up bits of me to send out to the outside world. My ideas, interests and passions are all shipped off, both to nourish the Patchwork House o Night and its guests.
The sweetmeat vendor is one of the few Patchwork people who are still awake.
I meet new people all the time
I'm offering parts of myself everyday
When would the vendor even be able to sleep?

Everyday we carve up and offer little parts of ourselves to the people around us. The Sweetmeat Vendor does it lovingly, taking parts of me and sending them out to nourish the rest of the Patchwork House of Night. My ideas, my thoughts and my vulnerabilities.
I held these close to my chest when I first came to University. I was petrified at the idea that I would have to show people these parts of myself.
Being an adult brings with it great freedom. And I believe this starts with the acceptance of the fact that it is okay and often necessary to let yourself be known.
I didn't have to put on airs or exclude myself. What got me through most of school wasn't necessary. I could, perhaps for the first time, just be myself.
To accept the fruits of love and growth, I had to give in to the mortifying ordeal of being known.

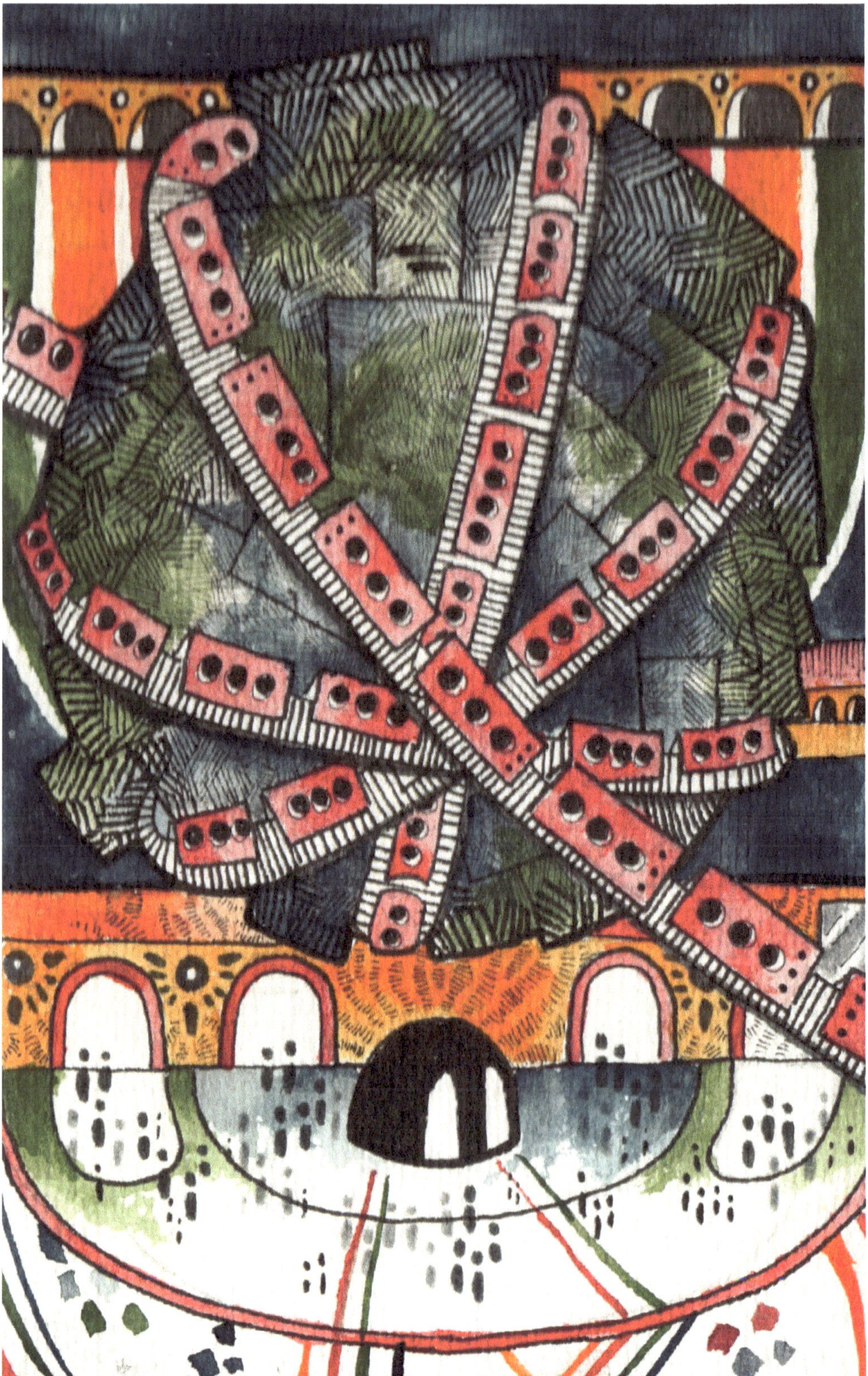

The Flyways

OCT 0 8 2022

There's that moment when it hits you, how free you are.
You can take the train of thought, board it at the Flyway station
You could go anywhere.
Adulthood promised me that I could go anywhere.
I was fortunate
I'd never felt so free before

Adulthood is Freedom.
That is what is promised anyway.
It was exhilarating. I was old enough to figure stuff out myself.
I boarded that train of thought and it took me to actions, adventures and people who I had previously never had the audacity to dream of.
I was growing, I was changing and I was moving.
These moments of freedom. The taste of independence. I chased after them.

On the heels of war and wonder
There's a stormy world up there
You can't whisper above the thunder
But you can fly anywhere

Purple burst of paper birds
This picture paints a thousand words
So take a breath of myth and mystery
And don't look back

From To The Sky by Owl City

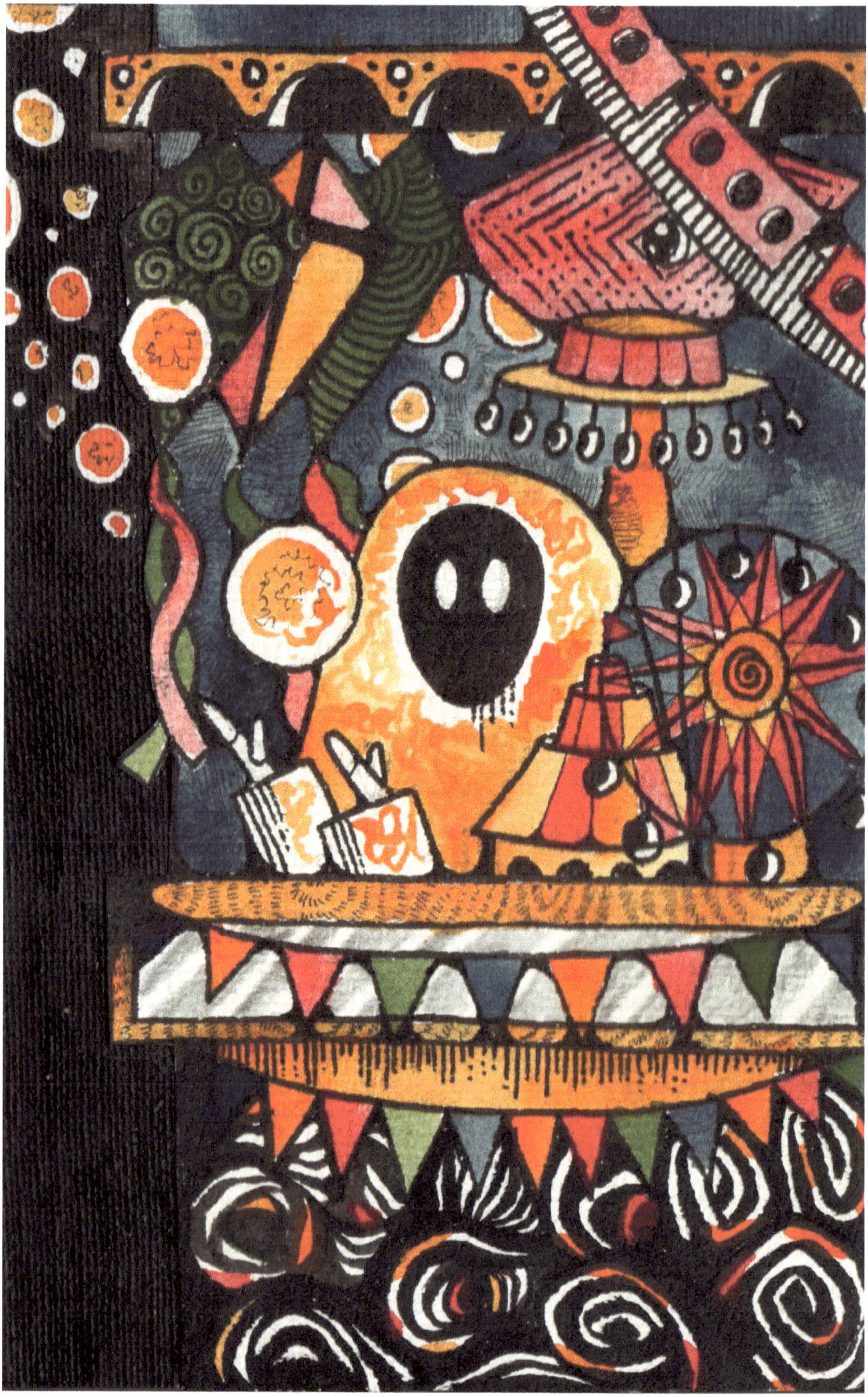

The Carnival

OCT 09 2022

Every day is a celebration.
The lantern keeper works tirelessly,
releasing lantern and firework into the air
around the Patchwork House of Night
We've come so far.
There's a lot to be joyful for
There's a lot to celebrate.

A lot of life is simply celebration.
There's an element of gratitude in there. An element of joy.
The Lantern Maker, alongside his brother the Sweetmeat vendor, work tirelessly to keep their guests happy.
They celebrate the beauty present all around the Patchwork House of Night.
We've come so far.
There's so much to celebrate.

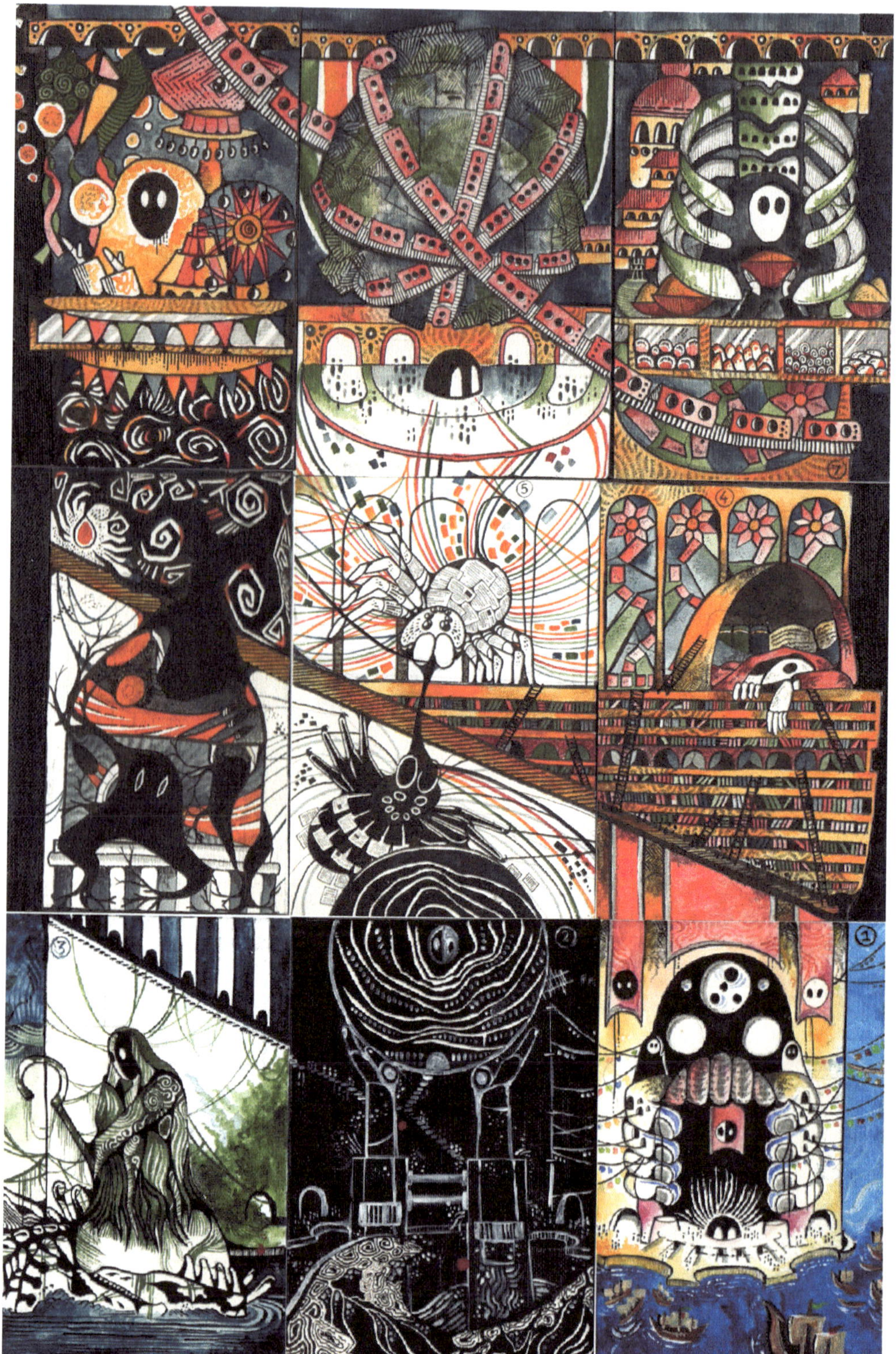
7
5
4
3
2
1

FREEDOM

“Years ago a friend of mine had a dream about a strange invention; a staircase you could descend deep underground, in which you heard recordings of all the things anyone had ever said about you, both good and bad. The catch was, you had to pass through all the worst things people had said before you could get to the highest compliments at the very bottom. There is no way I would ever make it more than two and a half steps down such a staircase, but I understand its terrible logic: if we want the rewards of being loved we have to submit to the mortifying ordeal of being known.”

-Tim Kreider

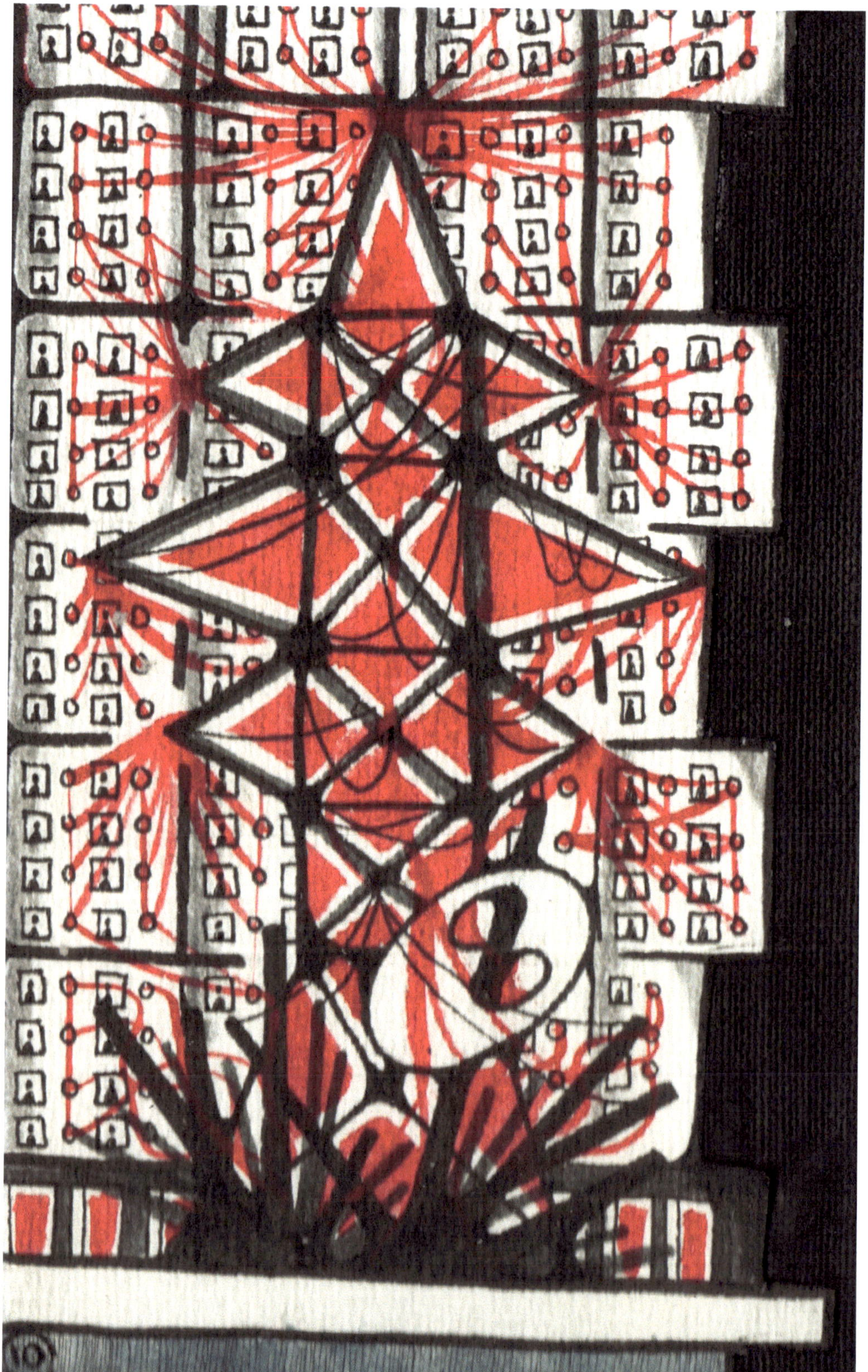

The Cubicles

OCT 10 2022

And the day after,

We go back to work
Line up in the cubicles, Power up the Patchwork House of Night.
There have been times in my life when I've been overworked, wires cross over and I'm all tangled up in my head
But all this stress must be worth something?
Right?

There's always work to do.
Bills to pay, stuff to study, work to do. The House of Night needs power.
Everyone has to put in a shift.

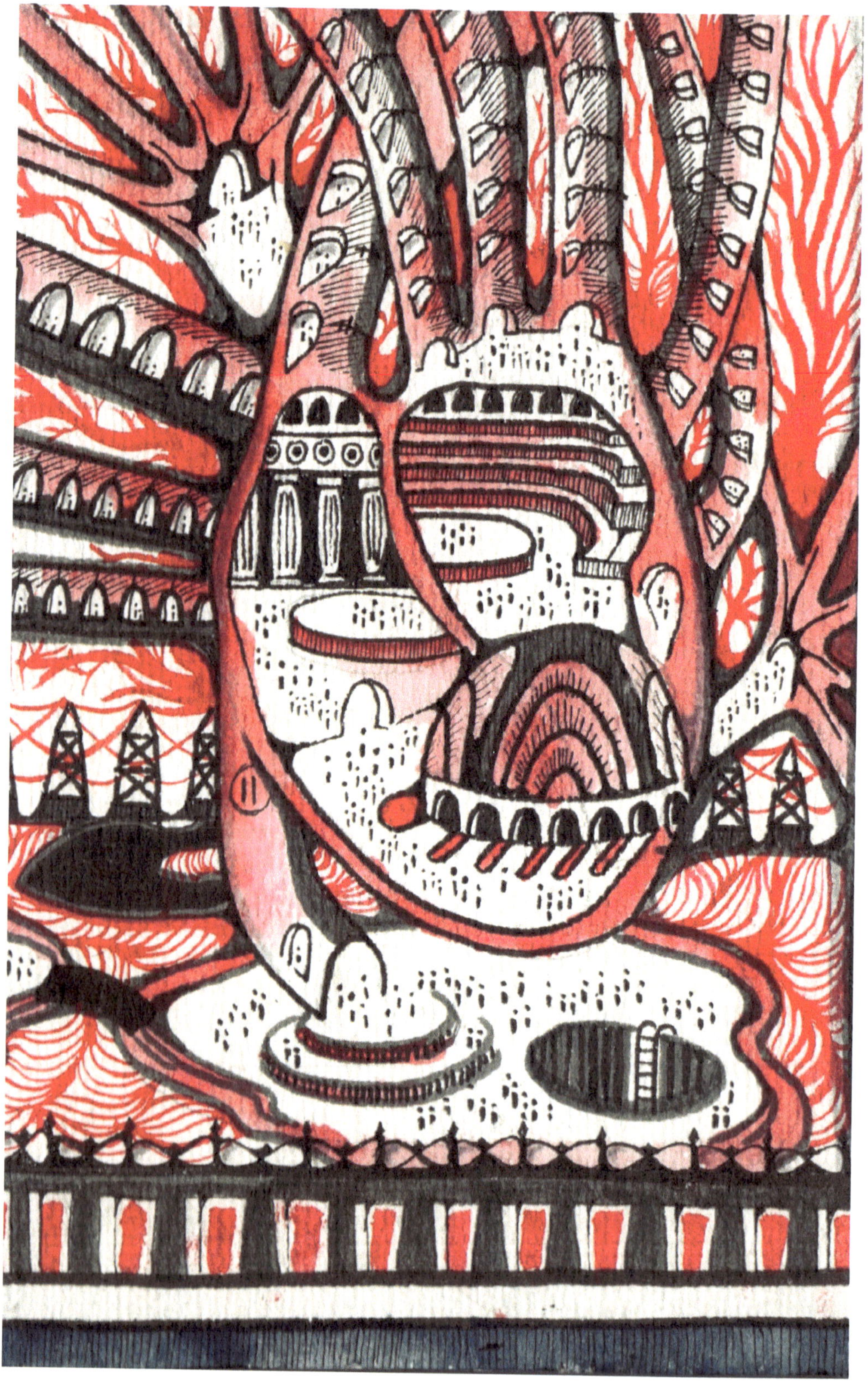

Heart Hall

OCT 11 2022

I contain multitudes
And everything about me passes through Heart Hall before circulating into the rest of the Patchwork House of Night.
It's always busy.
Meetings, Dramas, Revolts and Revolutions.
If you need something done, the council in the deepest part of the House needs to see it

The Patchwork House of Night is huge. It defies explanation. Most attempts at administrating happen at the Town Hall.
The literal heart of the megastructure, Heart Hall is an eclectic meeting ground of ideas, passions and conversations which swirl around its arteries and tunnels before finding their way to the rest of the House and the Mindlands.

"This city is a curse on cartographers
Bridges passing over bridges
Streets stacked upon streets upon streets
Parallel worlds that never quite meet"
....
And through our eyes, and hearts, and mouths
The city begins to know itself
Through our missed exits, bad calls, and wrong turns
It thoroughly, painstakingly, maps itself out

From "I think I'm going to leave my phone at home tonight" by the Narcissist Cookbook

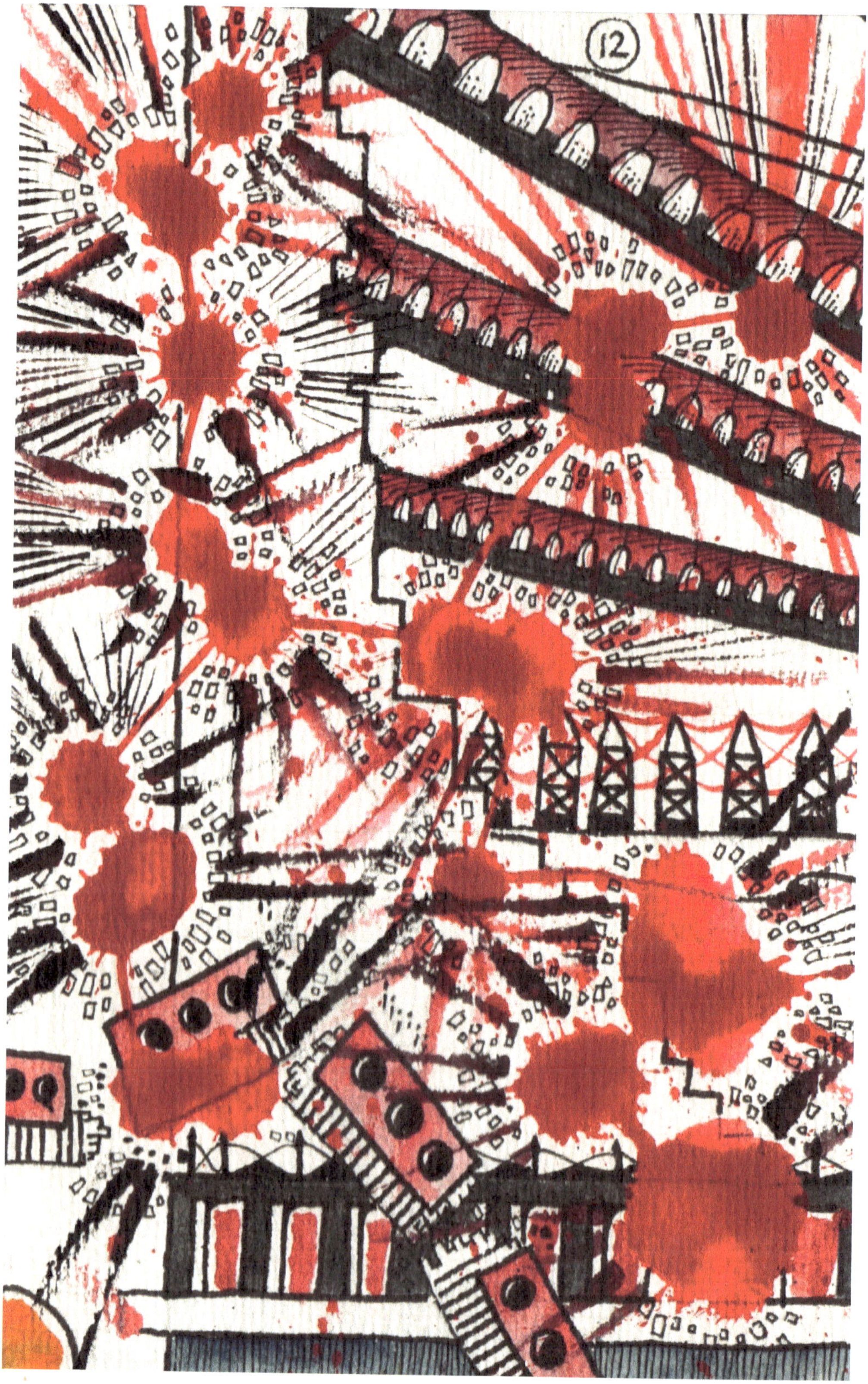
12

The Riots

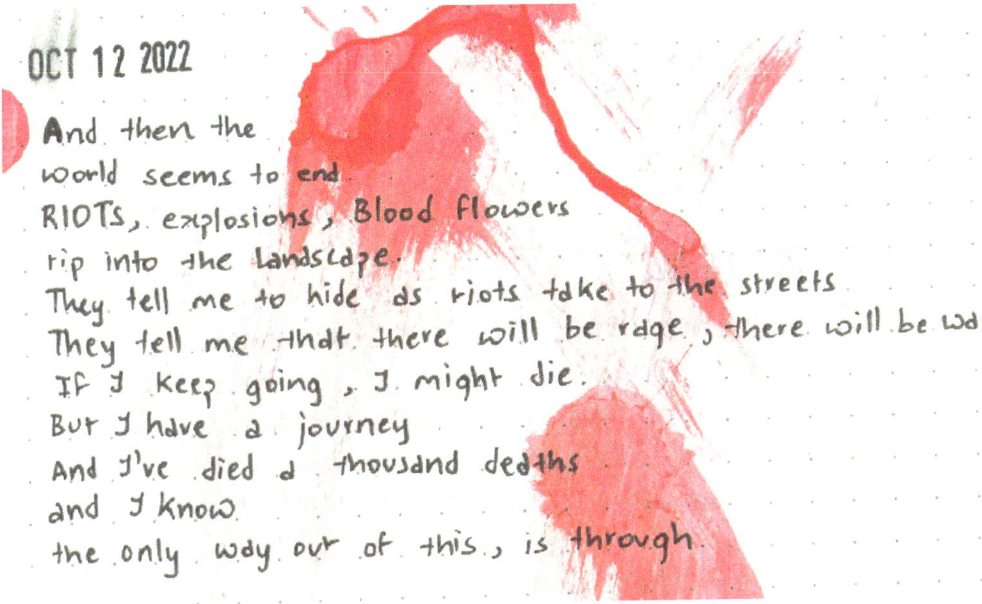

And when I walk into the parliament that is my own head. I face my thoughts. They clutch at their tattered banners. You can still faintly make out the hope written on them. Each time I see them I promise them that things will change. That this time, it will be different. This time, it will go differently.

And each time, I have lied to them.

and so they riot. They derail the train of thought. Explosions, hot as little suns and beautiful as blood flowers tear apart the Patchwork House of Night. They revel in its destruction because they know that there is something stronger than hope and it is fire and somethings truer than promises and they are ashes.

Anne Carson said "Why does Tragedy exist? Because you are full of rage. Why are you full of rage? Because you are full of grief"

The Riots will lead to war.

And I will stand aside. I cannot blame them. I let these thoughts, these feelings run their course.

And then I will pick up the pieces
and make new promises.

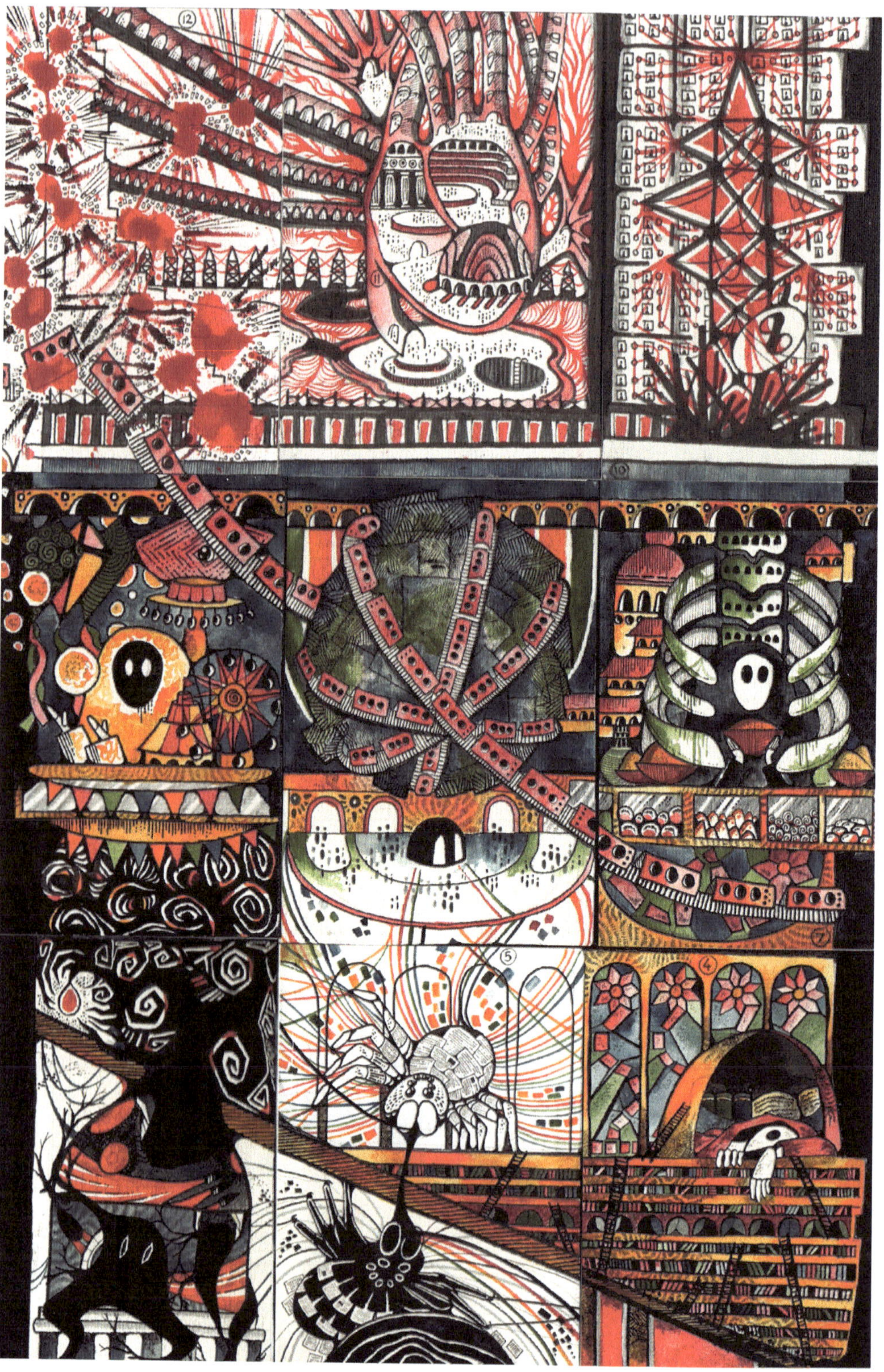

RESPONSIBILITY

"Working my money 'til I get gold
Monday-Friday mornin'
Working my money 'til I get gold
'Cause I can't get no more

Try to make a dollar out of 15 cents
But I ain't understand how the money was spent
My mama told me, "Boy you ain't got no sense
If we put it all together, can we pay this rent?"
I've been to some places, places I never should've been
I caught some changes, changes that made me who I am"

-From "Pure Grinding" by Avicii

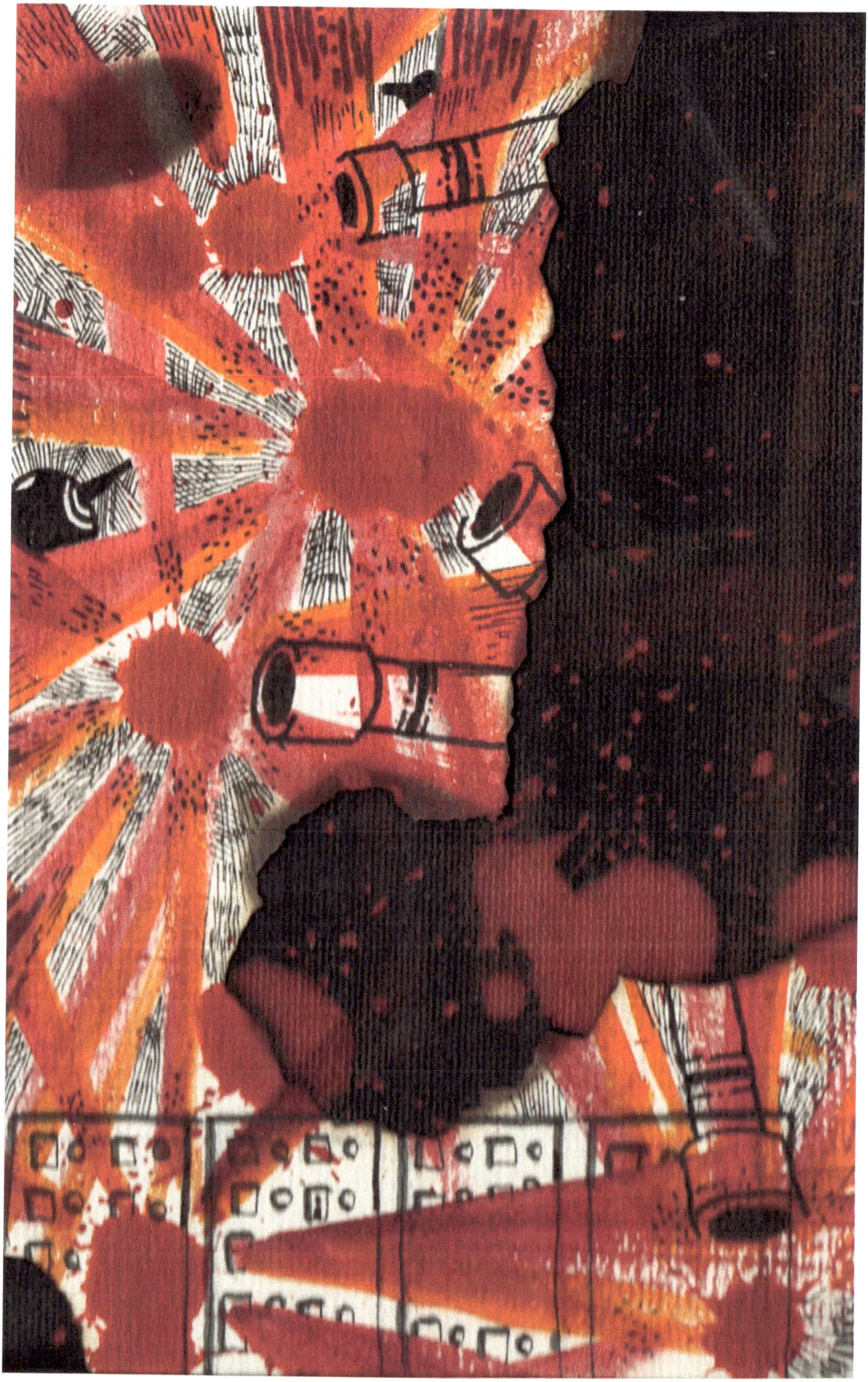

The War

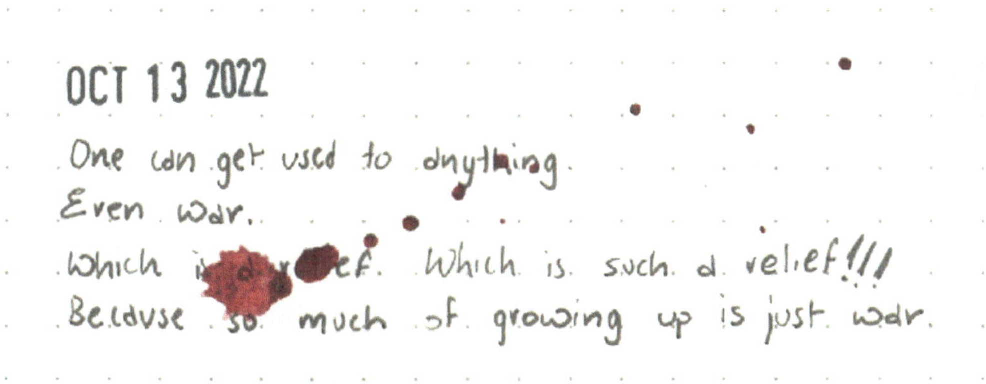

OCT 13 2022

One can get used to anything.
Even war.
Which i[illegible]ef. Which is such a relief!!!
Because so much of growing up is just war.

So much of growing up is war.
When thoughts war against themselves, they tear into the very structure and landscape of the House of Night.
A.I.T.A (Anti-Intrusive Thought Armament) guns go off all around me.
There's not much to say.
I can't be heard above the noise anyway.
I keep walking.

"My longing weeps for everything.
My longing shoots back at me,
to kill or be killed"

From "Another Road in the Road" by Mahmoud Darwish

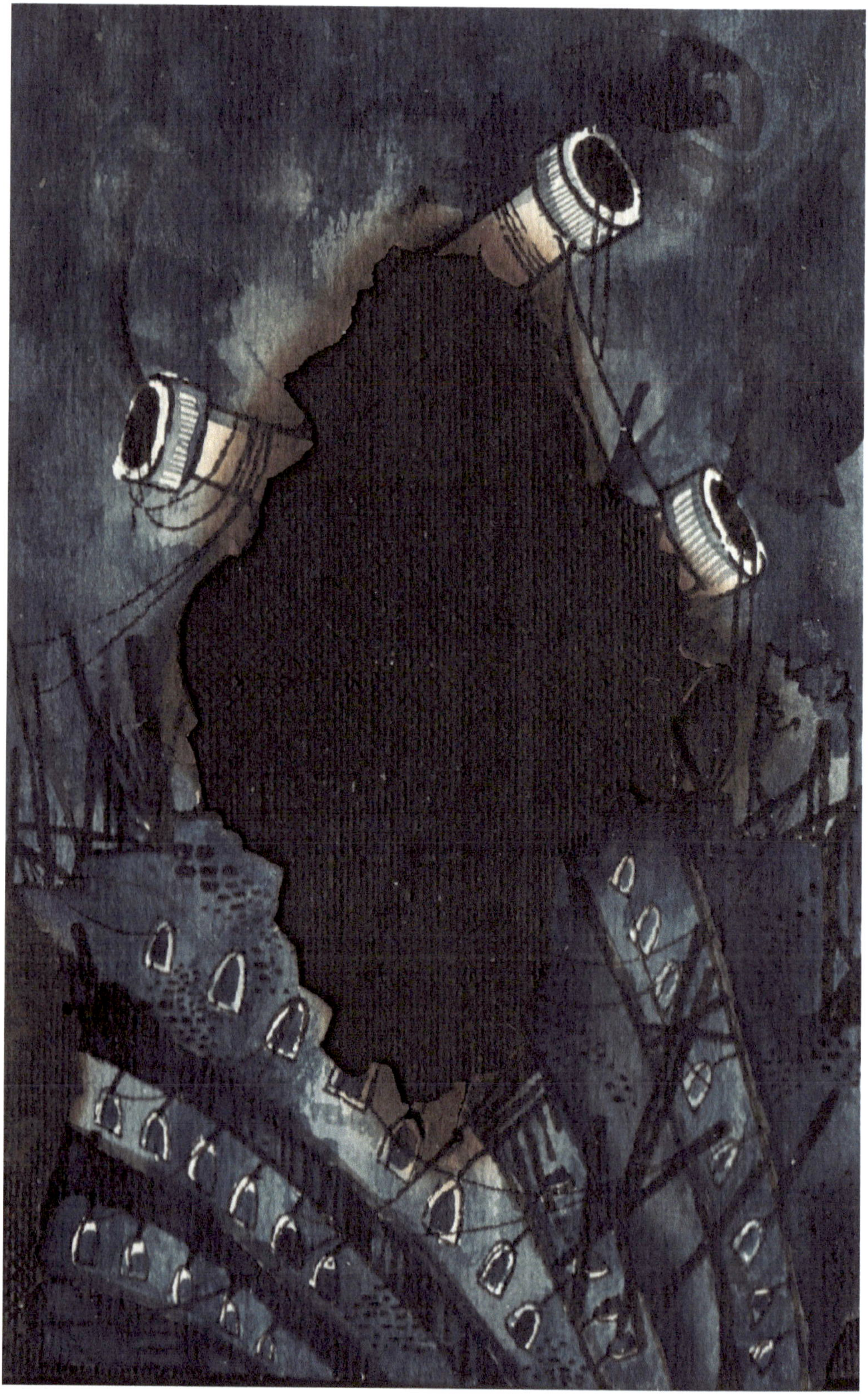

The Rubble

OCT 14 2022

There is a silence, a brief silence
between when the rubble has setted
and the mourning starts.
Maybe it only lasts long enough for a single breath
Just long enough to ask
"Have I survived?"
and knowing, wordlessly, that you have.

Not all of you will make it to adulthood.
This is simply how it is.
There are parts of you: traits, quirks, habits, memories that will erode, dissolve or be actively destroyed through the various wars that will plague your mind.
And the survivors will walk through the rubble.
But the parts of you that are dead never truly died. As Jon Banville said "We carry the dead with us only until we die too, and then it is we who are borne along for a little while, and then our bearers in their turn drop, and on into the unimaginable generations."
You arc your own descendant.
You are your own ancestor.
You have survived unimaginable generations.

"Ten spears go to battle" he whispered, "and nine shatter. Did the War forge the one that remained? No, Amaran. All the War did was identify the spear that would not break."

From "Oathbringer" by Brandon Sanderson

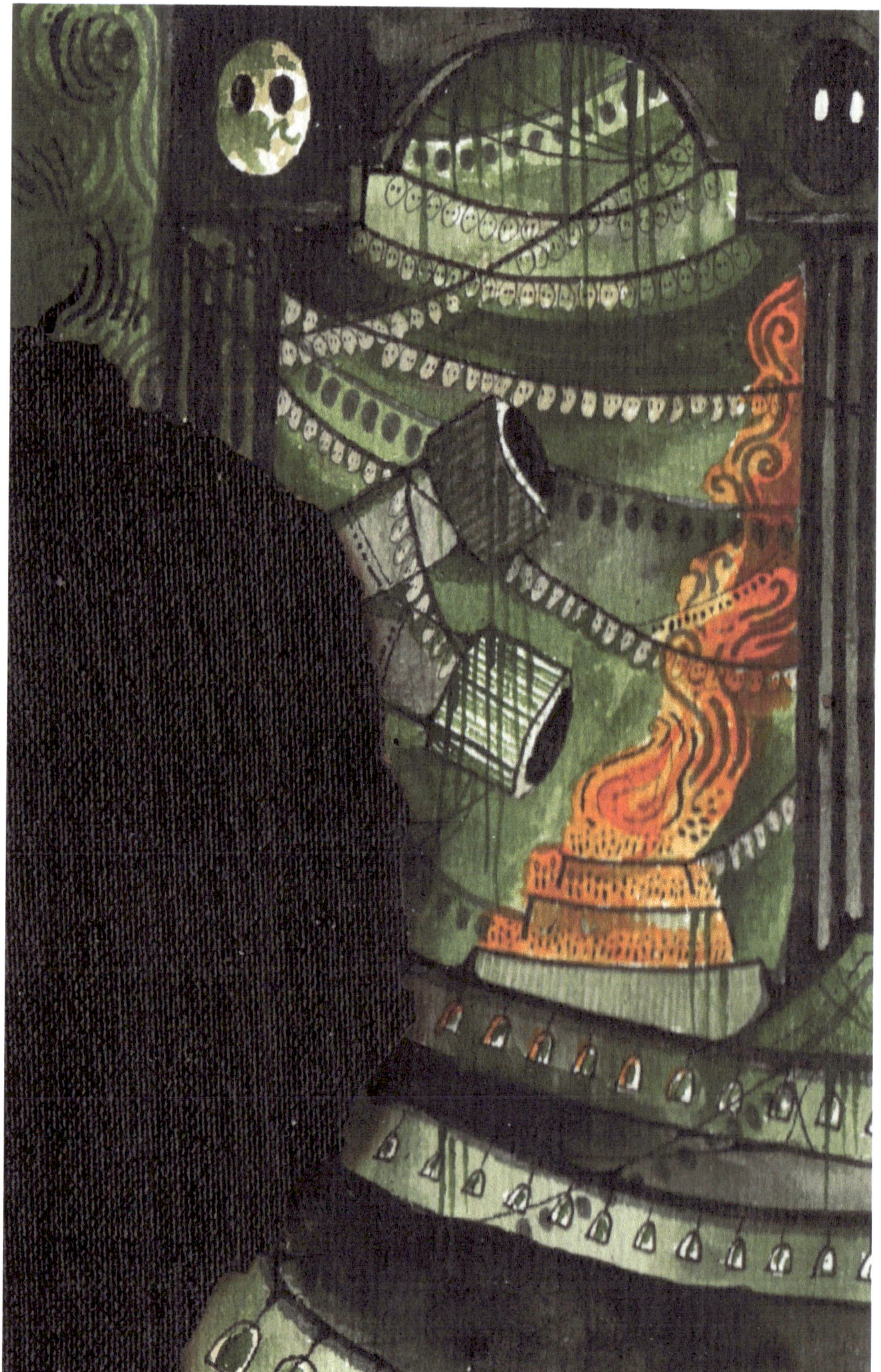

The Catacombs

OCT 15 2022

I visit the Altar in the catacombs
From it's arches are strung countless Masks
Remainders of the countless thoughts that
gave thier life in the service of the House.
I stay a while, watch the altar fire
simmer.
After all that loss
I might want to be alone for a while

When a Thought dies, its essence is broken down immediately, recycled and it passes back into the Mindlands and the House of Night.
When a Thought dies in the service of the Patchwork House of Night, it leaves behind a mask that is strung up by the Catacombs.
Row after row of millions of fading, moss covered masks stretch onwards into eternity, surrounding a smoldering flame.
People come by to pay their respects.
Those who carry on walking up the Patchwork House of Night after seeing how much has been lost....they too get a little lost.

"What do sad people have in common?
It seems that they have all built a shrine to the past
and often go there and do a strange wail
and worship.
What is the beginning of happiness
It is to stop being so religious like that"

Hafez

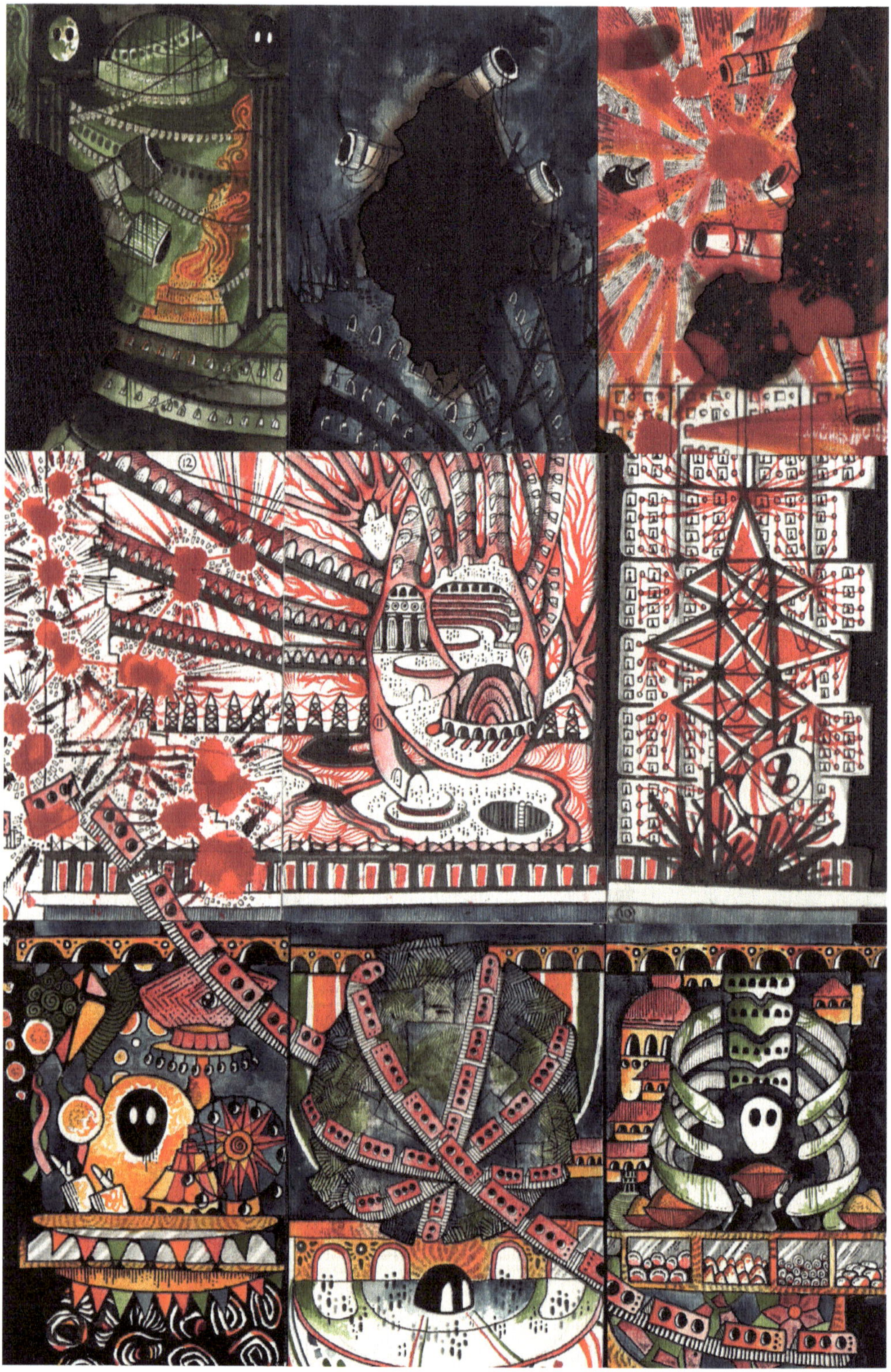

Loss

"All my grief says the same thing:
this isn't how it's supposed to be.
this isn't how it's supposed to be.
and the world laughs
holds my hope by my throat.
says:
but this is how it is"

-Fortesa Latifi

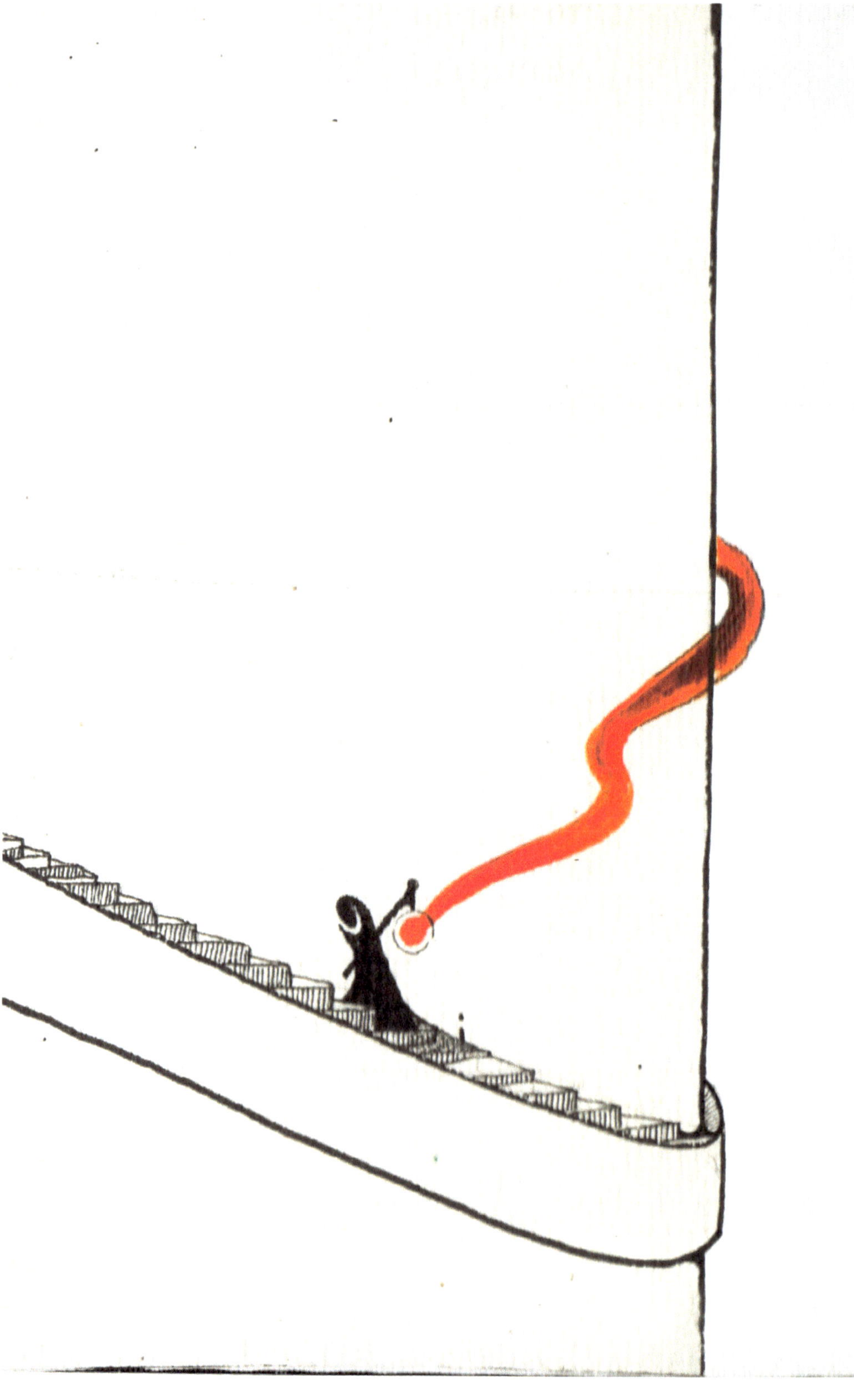

Hello?

OCT 16 2022

"Hello?"

My question echoes out.

I'm met by a figure in a faceless mask. It holds a lantern and I follow it.
It doesn't say a word.
I look out into the void around the towering House. It is white and cloudy here.
I call out a greeting and it hurtles into the nothingness.
And as I walk onwards,
I wait for an answer

"The most beautiful part of your body
is where it's headed.
& remember,
loneliness is still time spent with the world.

-From "Someday I'll love Ocean Vuong" by Ocean Vuong

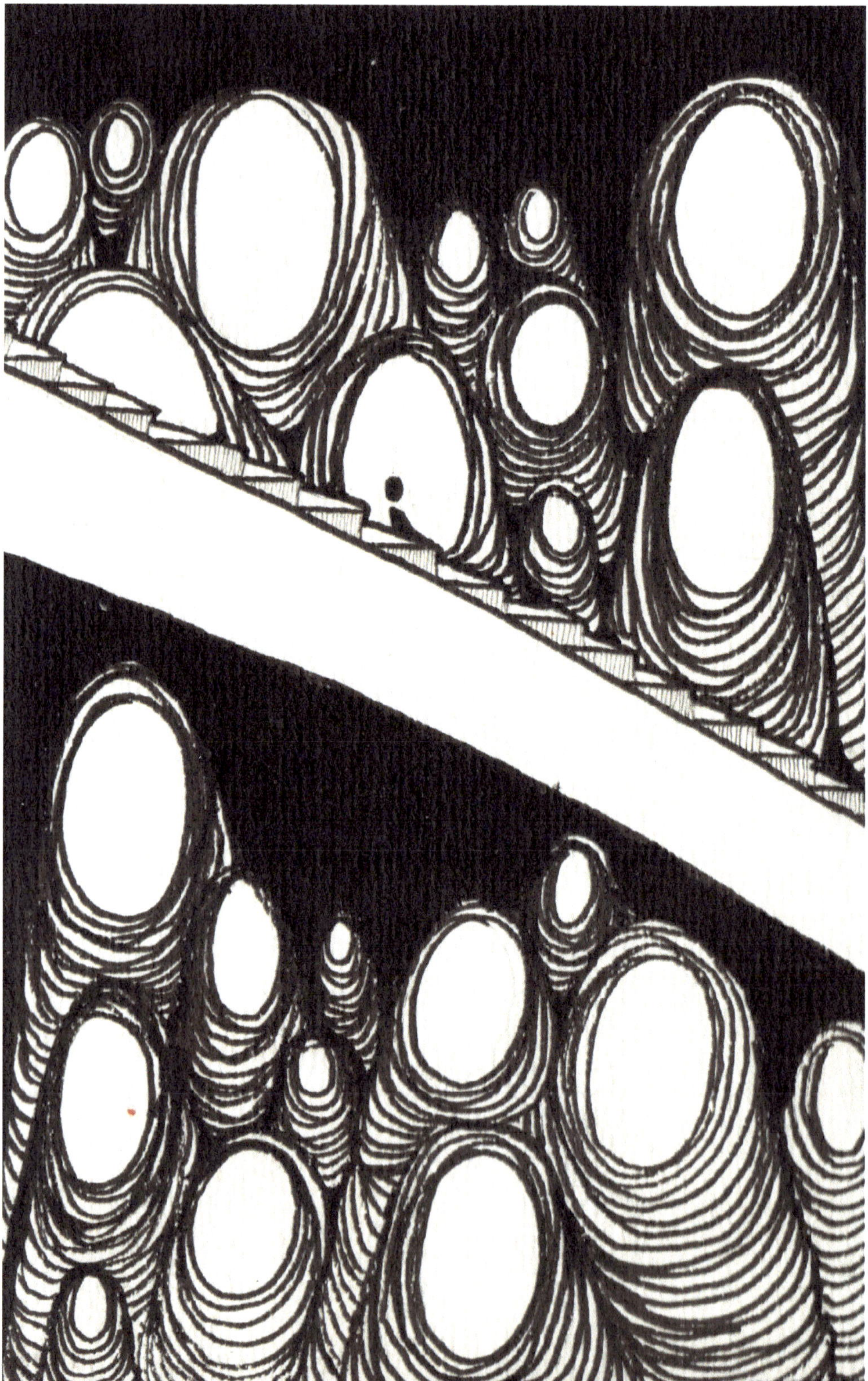

OCT 1 7 2022

They murmur.
Row after row of faceless masks.
They don't notice me. I don't mind.
I hear snatches of what they're saying.
Snippets of lives, so close yet so far removed from my own.
I feel loneliest in crowds. All of us, ships passing in the night.
If there's one comfort I take from that metaphor it is that every ship is going somewhere.
I can only hope it isn't the bottom of the sea.

"I love the crowd as I love the sea.
And despite the crush and the noise,
I don't mind diving into the crowd.
Not to be engulfed by or lost in it....
but to sail it like a solitary pirate,
seeming to follow its rhythm...
but finding my own when the current breaks
or dissipates.
Like the sea, a crowd is invigorating.

-From "L'amour l'apres midi, 1972" by Eric Rohmer

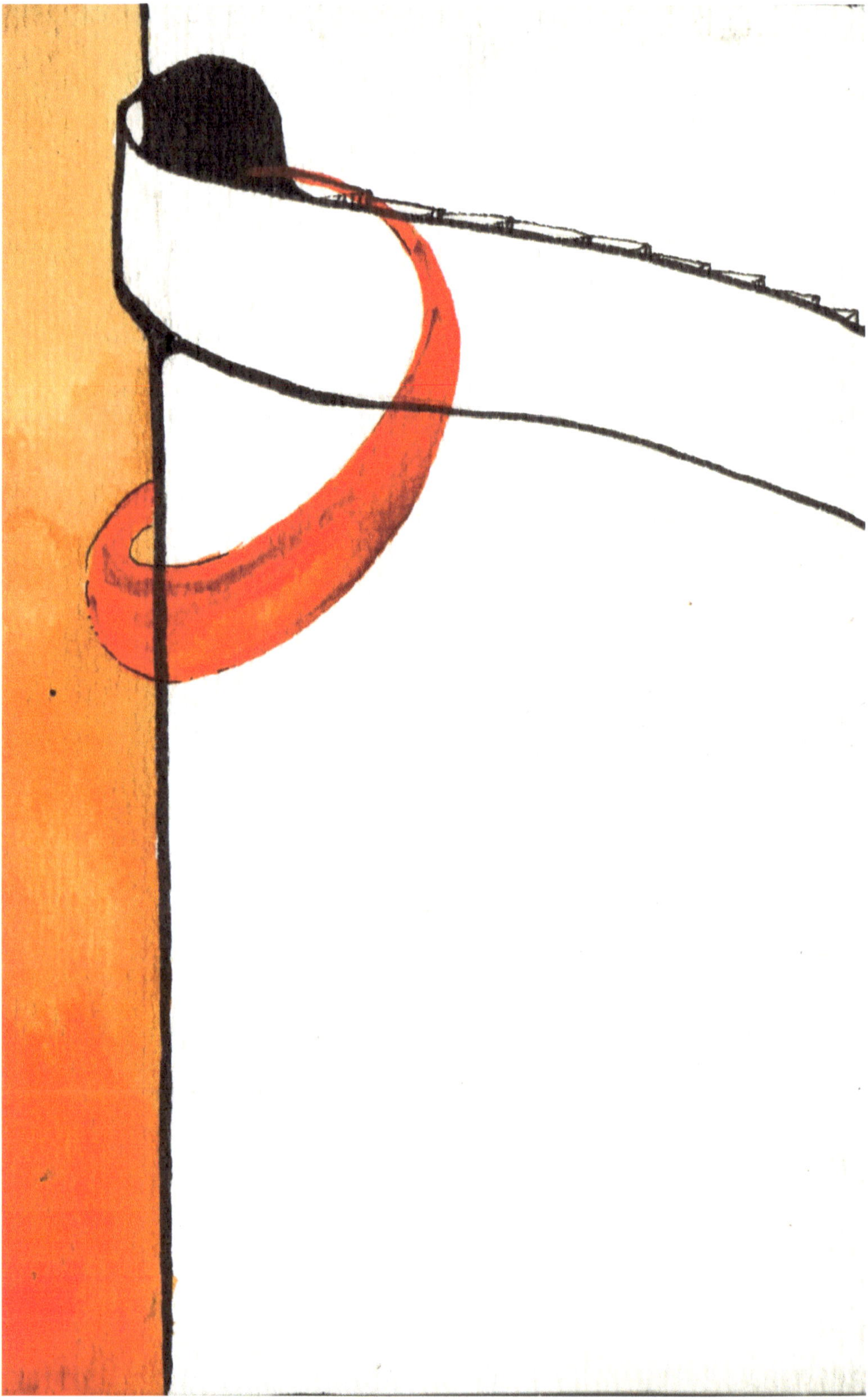

Goodbye.

OCT 18 2022

"Goodbye"
The answer echoes back.

I could stay.
I don't have to turn the corner. I don't have to keep walking. I can keep my own company and watch the endless, unchanging orange sky.
There is comfort in loneliness.
But I don't stay.
I have things I need to do
and faces I need to fall in love with
so I walk on.

"I'm used to being lonely
but forever to be a stranger
is a strange grief."

-From "The Unknown Continent" by Ursula K. Le Guin

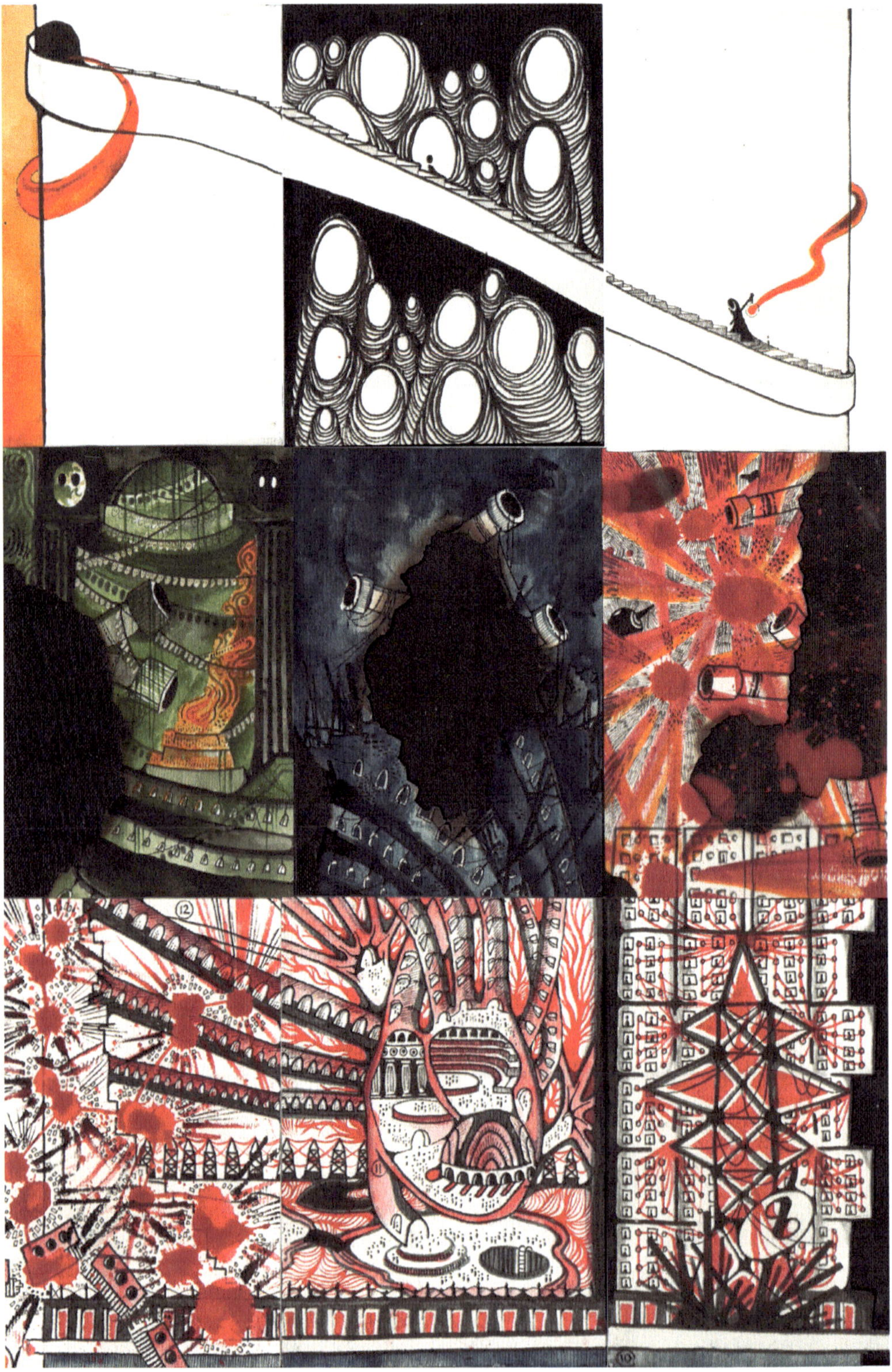

LONELINESS

The Lonely is one of the Entities. It is a manifestation of the fear of isolation, of being completely cut off and alone, the fear of being disconnected. Victims are generally either predisposed to isolation or simply have the misfortune to cross paths with the Lukas family. The Lonely often manifests as fog, ships, travel and faceless crowds.

-The Magnus Archives

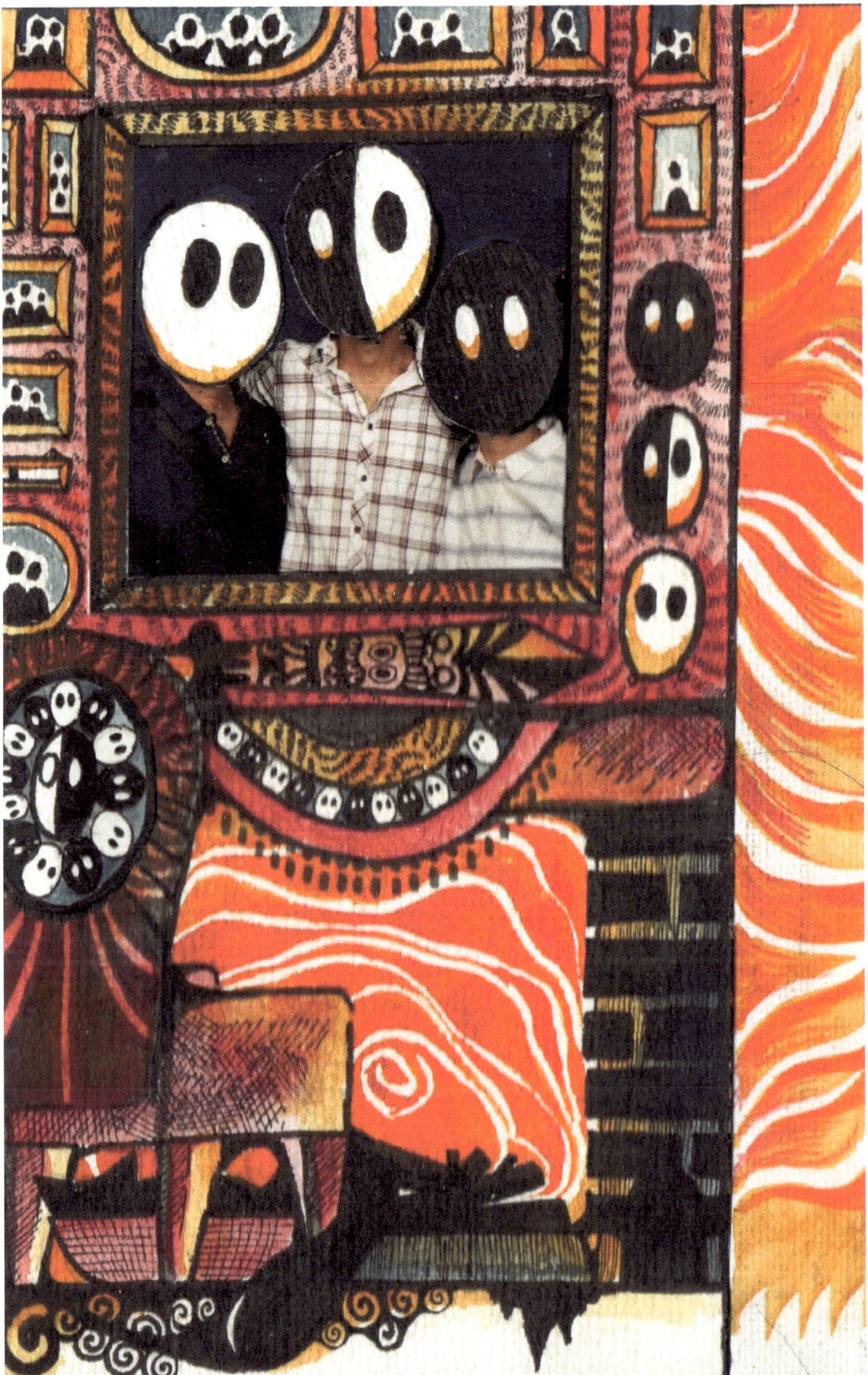

The Hearth

OCT 19 2022

I'm tired.
So now I go to the hearth, I seek out the warmth
I go home ...
to the people who loved me
long before I could even ask for it.

I'm tired.
And maybe everything is a little too much.
So I'll go home, to my family
And though my childhood room is now a study, and my childhood bed is now a desk...
I'm still their child.
I'm older, wiser and wearier but God
I'm still their child.

"All my life
I've never known where you've been
There were holes in you
The kind that I could not mend
And I heard you say
Right when you left that day
"Does everything go away?"
Yeah, everything goes away
But I'm going to be here 'til forever
So just call when you're around "

From "Always Gold" by Radical Face

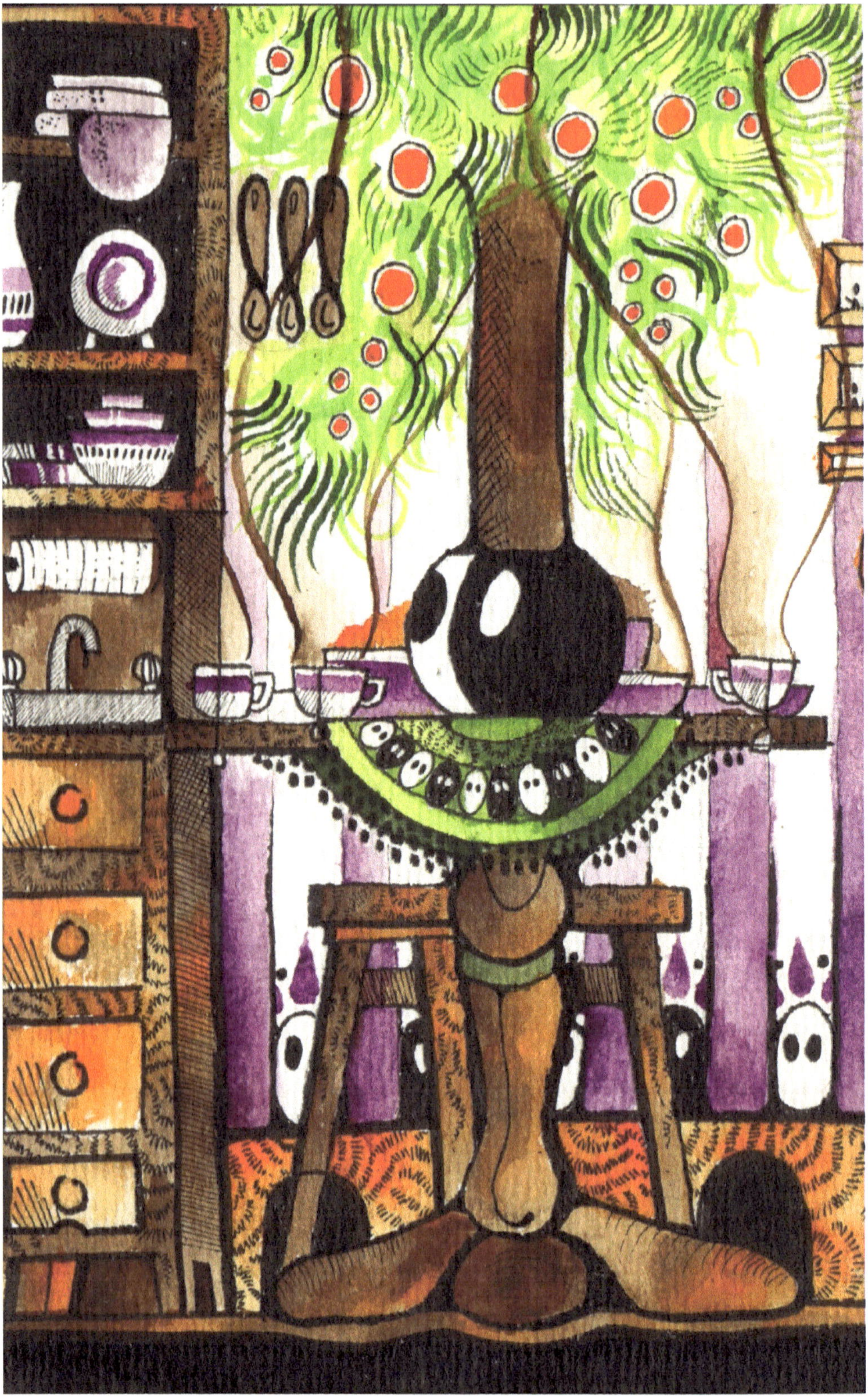

The Kitchen

OCT 20 2022

I can't grow until I eat.
And at the Patchwork House, we never eat alone
Disagreements, ideas, troubles and worries melt away over
hot food and freshly unhungry stomachs.
Food is better when we share it with those we love.
I imagine growing up to be much the same.

My heart has healed a hundred times over the dining table. My hands have shared countless morsels.
I've been countless people over my life
and they've all needed to be fed.
Here, at the Patchwork House of Night
No one eats alone.

"Perhaps the world will end at the kitchen table,
while we are laughing and crying,
eating of the last sweet bite.

From "Perhaps the World Ends Here" by Joy Harjo

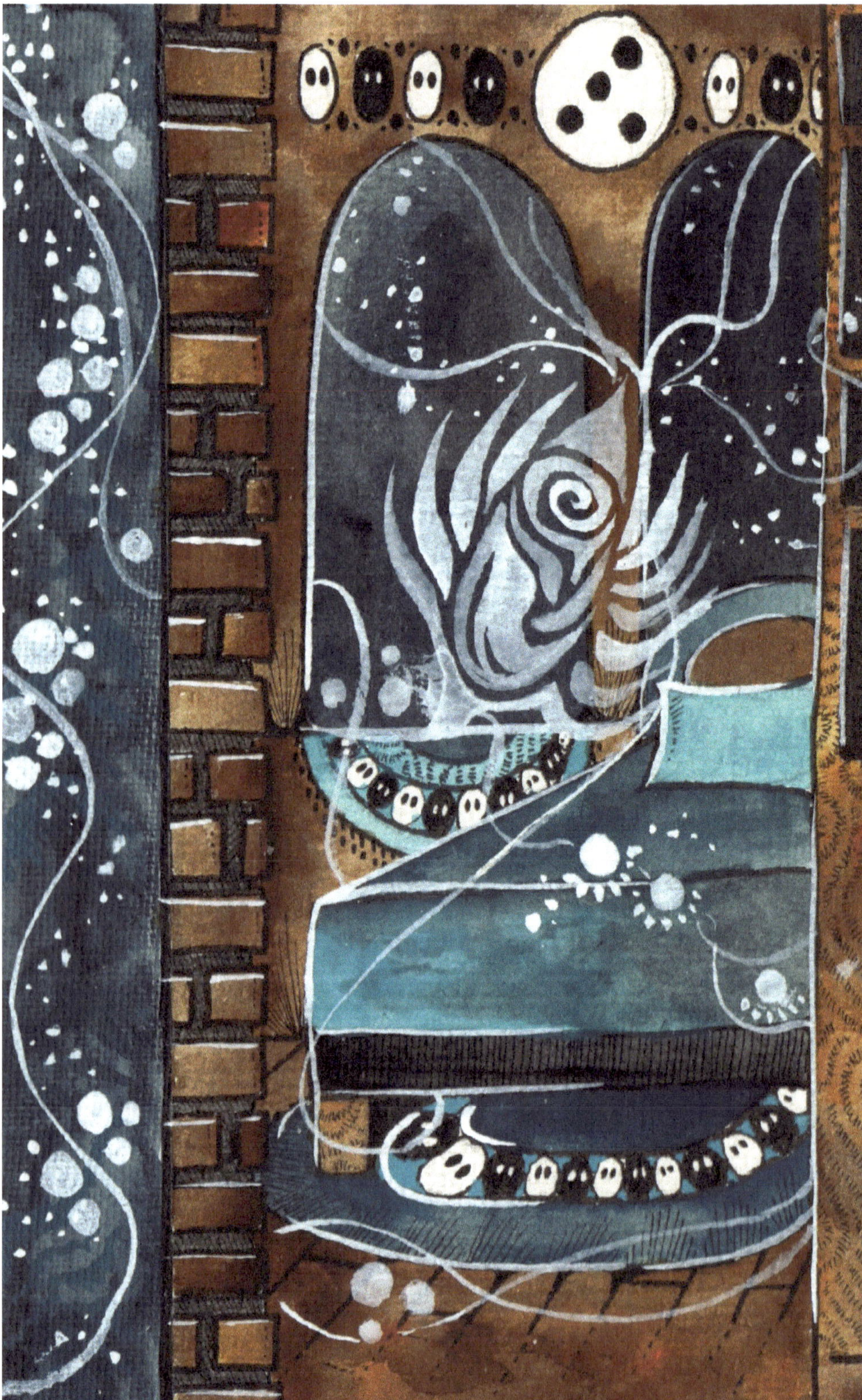

The Window

OCT 21 2022

And the last thing I need to rest is a
good night's sleep.
My childhood room, a part of the Patchwork House
that is unimaginably old, is covered in Moonflowers.
And why would'nt it be?
Did I not sit by the window as a child and tell the
moon stories of the life I would have? the people I'd
meet?
And today, when I come back to rest
the moon greets me with flowers and says
"I love you, look how far you've come, stay a while,
rest a while, tell me stories like you used to"
"I've missed you"

Growing up, I'd sometimes wake up in the dead of night and go sit by the window.
I'd stare at the night sky and talk out loud to the moon.
The moon is sacred in the Mindlands. Deep in the subconscious wilds are moonflowers that can cure any ailment of the heart or spirit.
My childhood room, as I see it in my head, is overrun with moonflowers.
All those years I spent dreaming there.
You cannot find more fertile ground.

"If someday the moon calls you by your name
don't be surprised, because every night
I tell her about you"

-Shahrazad al Khalji

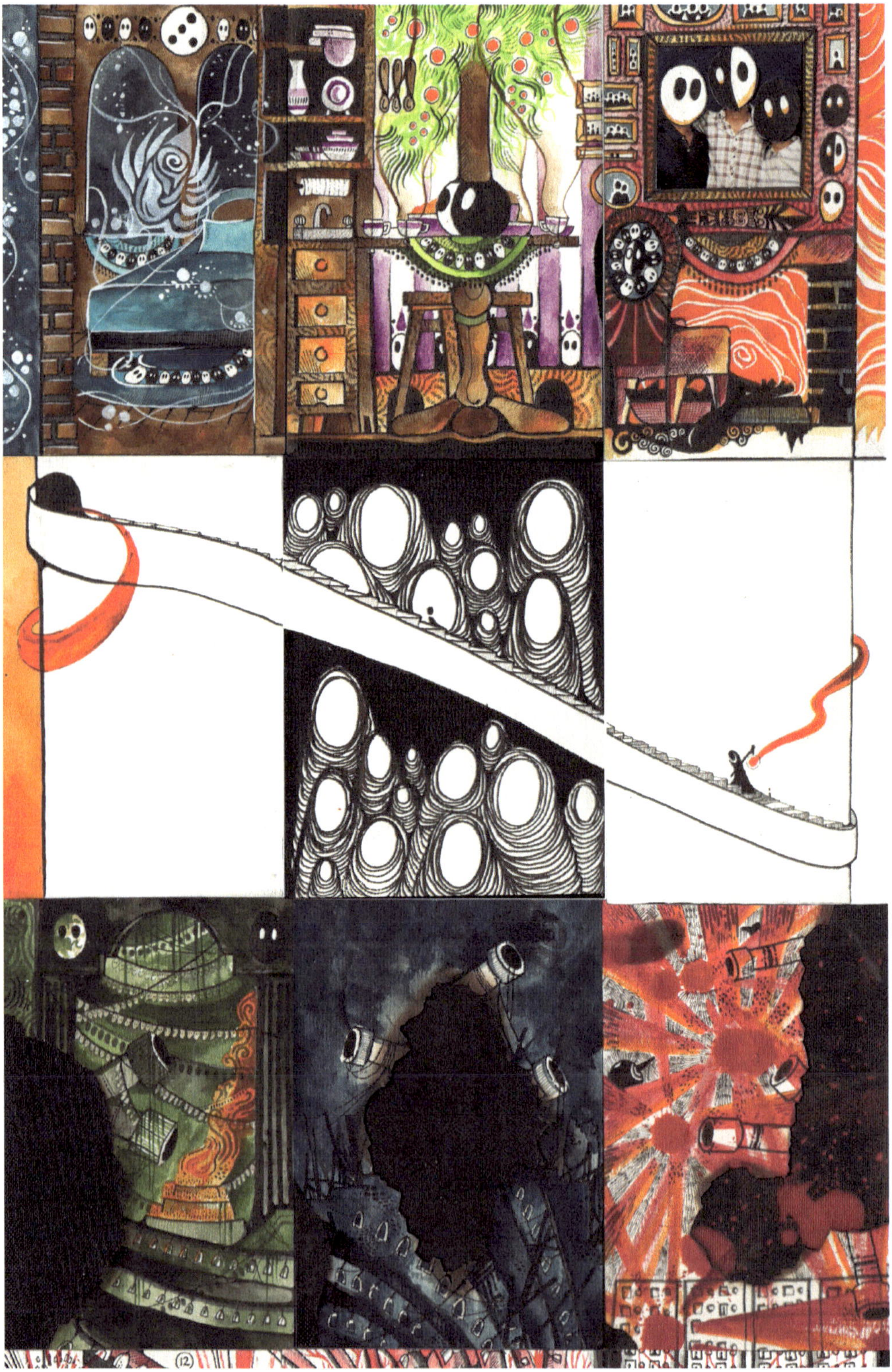

NOSTALGIA

And all my travels seem to bring me back to this place
And all my life I've just been looking for the right way
And I've been thinking to myself that this is who I gotta be
And I've been jivin' on my own to find the right pace
And I've been watching all the clocks, I need the timeframe
I wonder when will come the day, I wonder when I'll see those dreams
....
And all my travels seem to bring me back to this place
But all my life I've just been looking for the right way
And I've been thinking to myself that this is who I gotta be

-From "Travels" by Khai Dreams

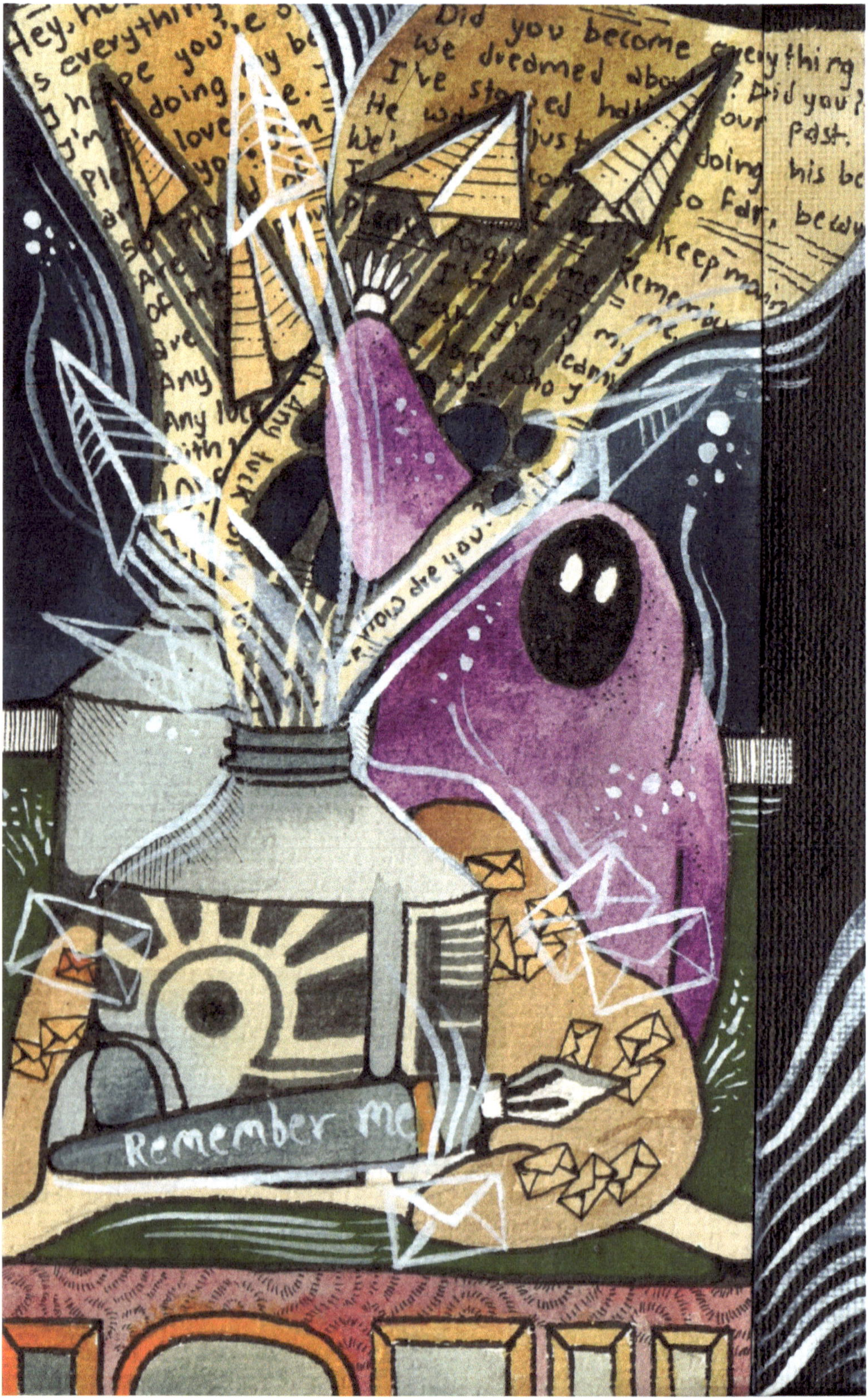
Did you become
Remember me

The Post Office

OCT 22 2022

The Patchwork House of Night's Post office is always busy. The Postal lad folds the letters they recieve and send them flying out into the world.
I've written so many letters, so many to myself.
I ask myself how I'm doing. whether I'm eating well
whether I'm sleeping well, dreaming well.
whether I've had any luck with love yet?
And as I send these questions out into my future, I go back to my life and try to make happy answers to them.

I think everyone should write a letter. I highly recommend it. I also think people should write letters to themselves.
A letter used to unite the world across unimaginable distances. A letter to oneself is the closest thing to time travel we can get.
And when I hear the questions I had back then, I wish I could go back and tell little old me all that I've since learned.

"Write that down. I AM VERY YOUNG
AND I AM LEARNING HOW TO LIVE
Tape it to the wall by your bed and read it
every morning.

You are very, very young.
You are learning how to live.

-Heather Havrilesky

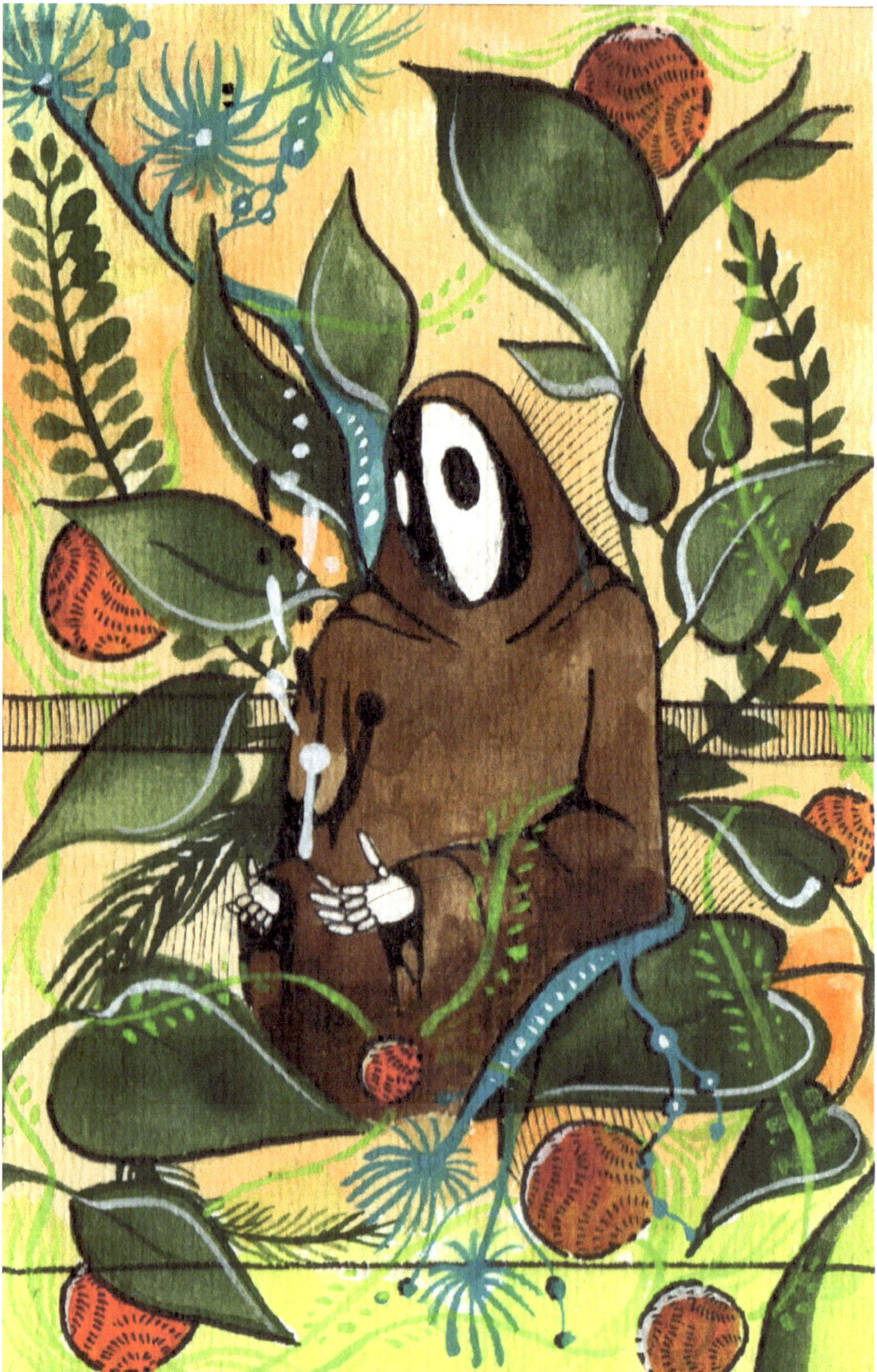

The Garden

OCT 23 2022

The Garden is lush. The Gardener tends to it tirelessly
Every thing I've ever been started as a seed of a
thought. It started here
The Gardener keeps copius, reservoirs of seed in case
I'm ever struck by famine or catastrophe.
I will never completely die
and one day when my body does go still, it'll
break off into the universe
which is a garden in it's own right if you think
about it.

Citizens of the Patchwork House of Night make routine visits to the Garden. They go there to rest, recuperate and remember who they are. Perhaps fantasize about who they might become. And when the House is wracked by war or famine, loneliness or trauma, the Garden grows quietly. The Gardener is ready at a moments notice to send out seeds and repopulate the Mindlands in the event of a calamity. There is hope in every leaf, fruit and flower in the Garden. There is hope in every person who goes through it.

It has brought me back from death countless times in the past and will continue to do so for years to come.

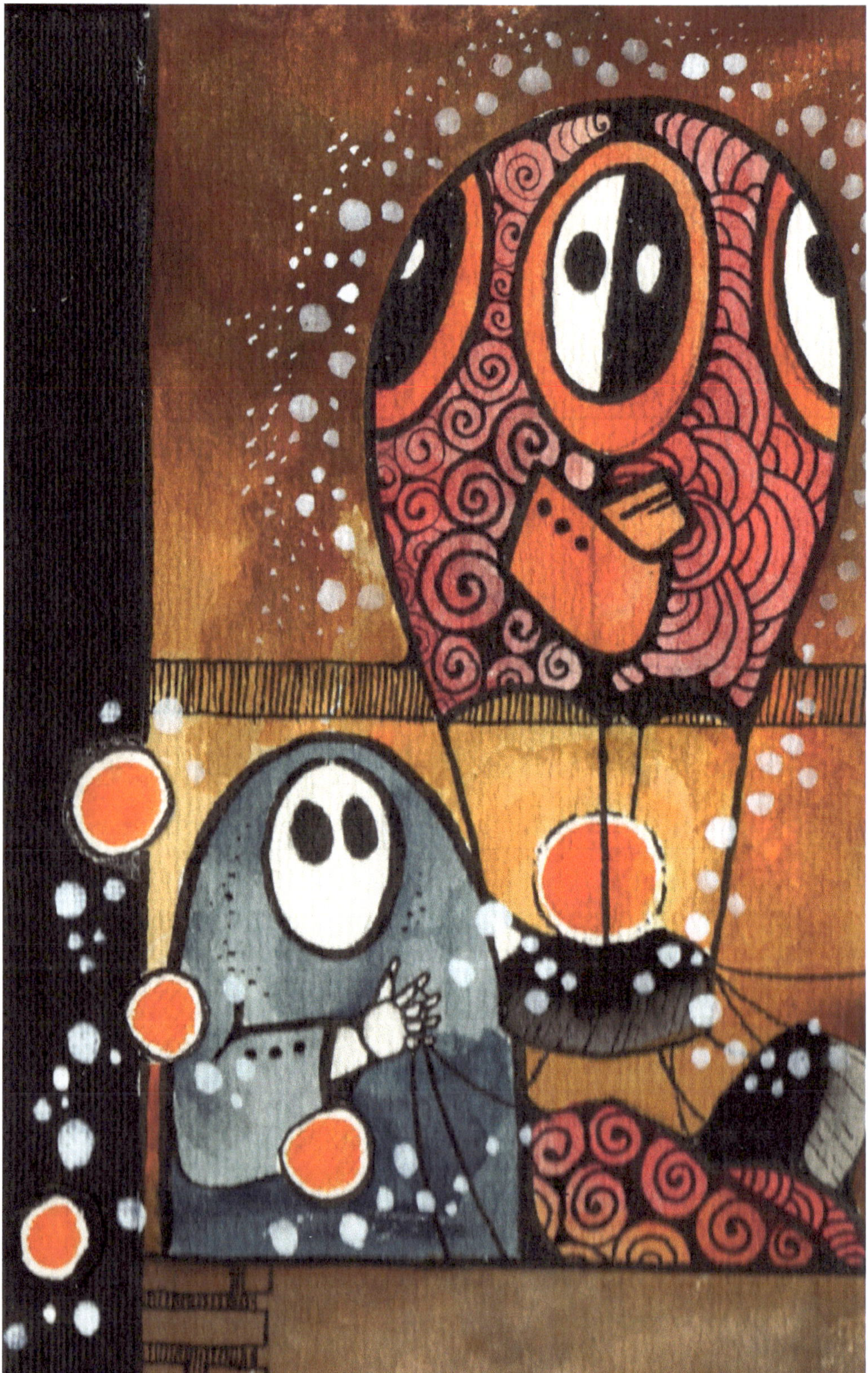

The Lanterns

OCT 24 2022

Lanterns!! The same ones sent up from many floors below
whilst they may have once stood for celebrations,
they now stand for hope.
And is'nt that the way of things, we take the
light of all the happy things we once saw as
ecstatic proof that there is yet more light to come!!

We've released Lanterns once before. It was to celebrate. Isn't there so much to celebrate? But now we release Lanterns in the hope that there will be more to celebrate in the days to come.

The Patchwork Person who releases these lanterns takes our hope into the future, punctuating the endless night sky with floating stars and, for a beautiful brief moment, writing out entire new constellations for me to write meaning into.

"Come on, dance with me.
The earth is spinning.
We can't just stand on it."

-Dino Ahmetovic

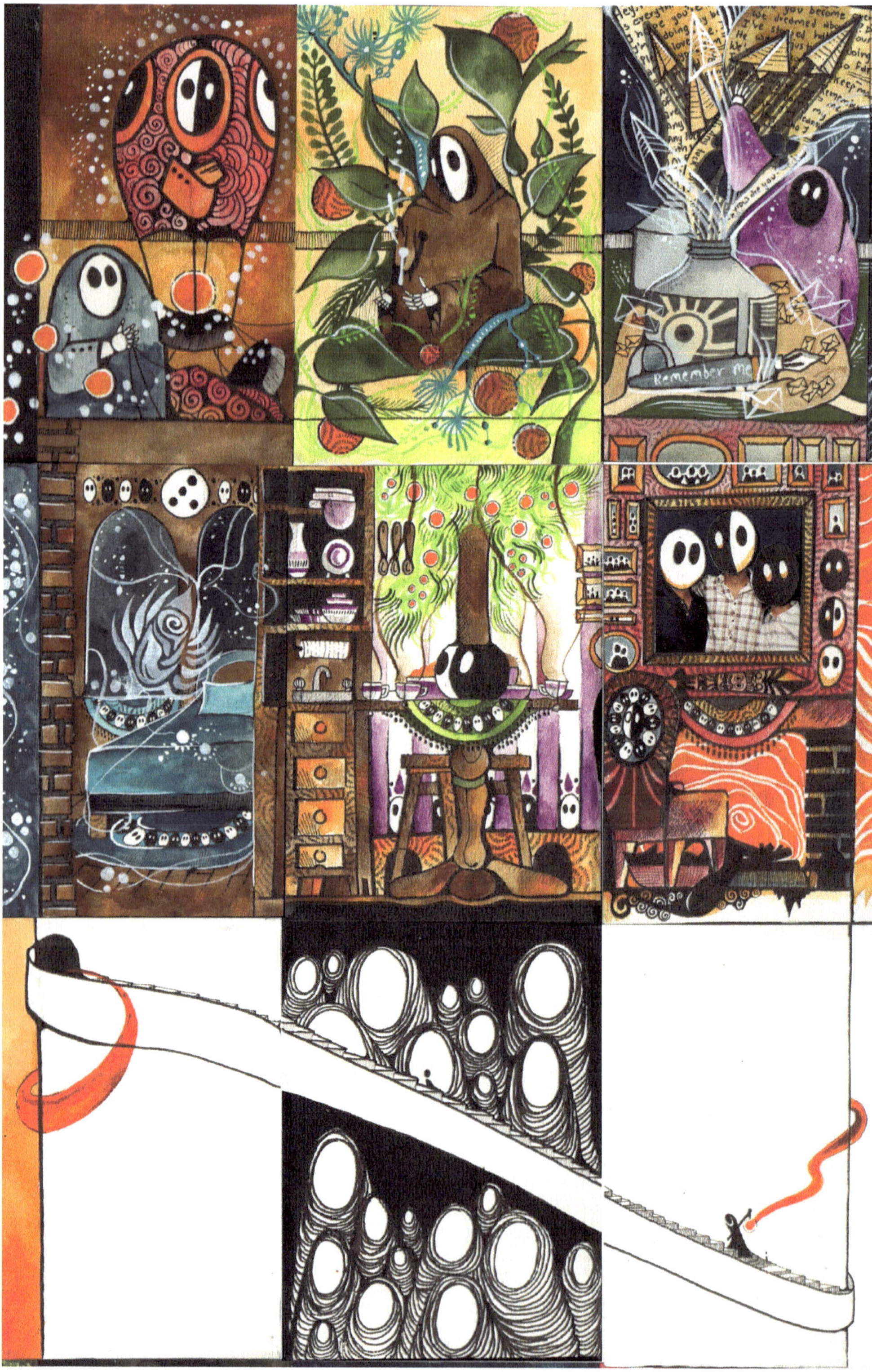
Remember me

HOPE

In the dark times
Will there also be singing?
Yes, there will also be singing
about the dark times.

-Bertolt Brecht

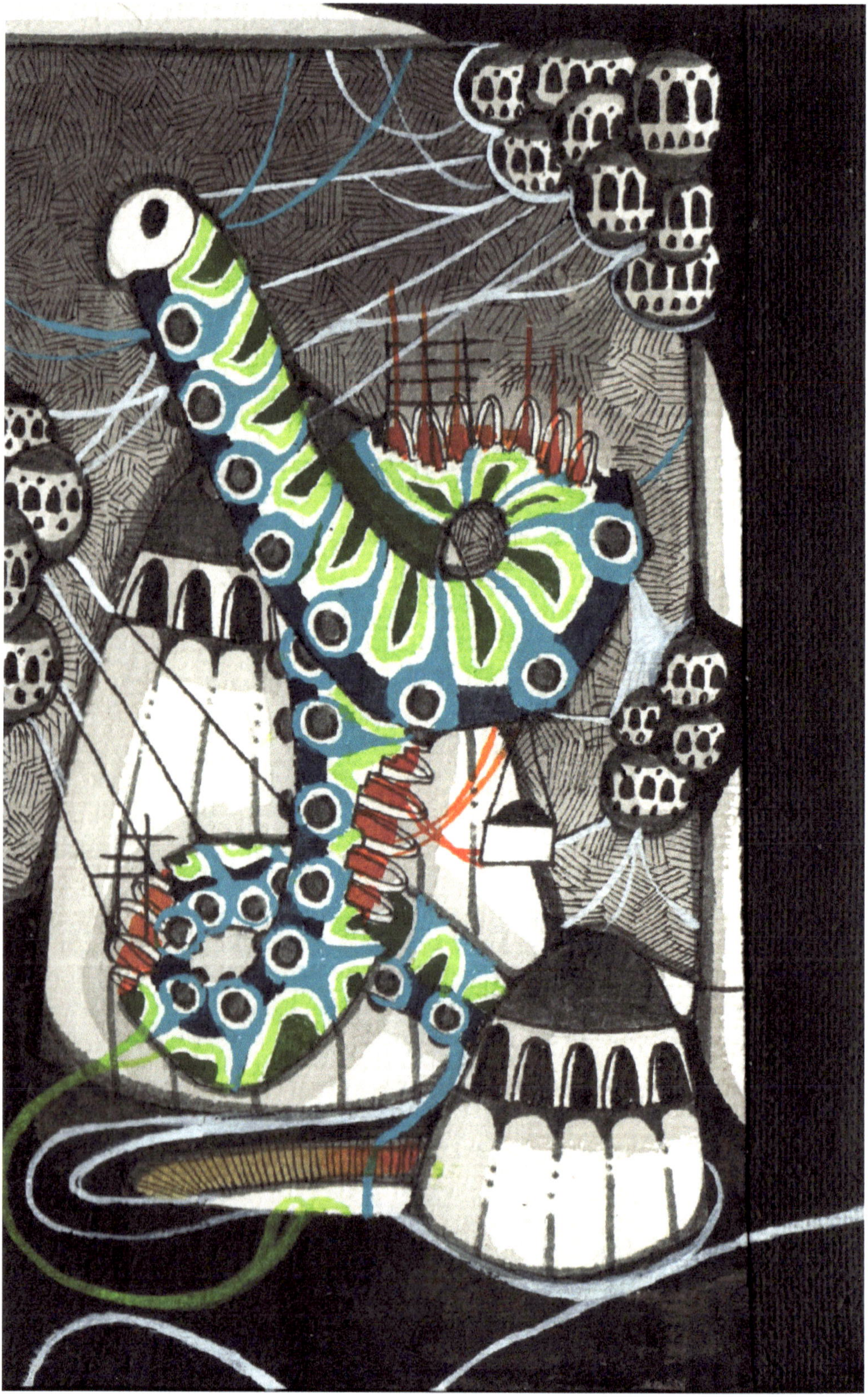

The Architect

OCT 25 2022

We've almost at the end now
The **top of the House** is generally under construction.
After stewing on the way my life has been and is for so many floors,
I should give some thought to what will come to be.

The Patchwork House of Night is always under construction. It is never complete. Even as I'm laid down to rest, it will continue to build itself floor by floor (though I won't be the one doing the building then).
Every new floor starts with the Architect. A plan, a rough sketch that allows for the various thoughts working round the clock to lift themselves up.

"i crawl in the moss, it is easy to find god.
she is a cluster of eels beneath my palms.
i ask of her, am i doing any of this life right?
and she, with her many mouths,
says nothing."

-From "Outbreaks" by Kitchen Mckeown

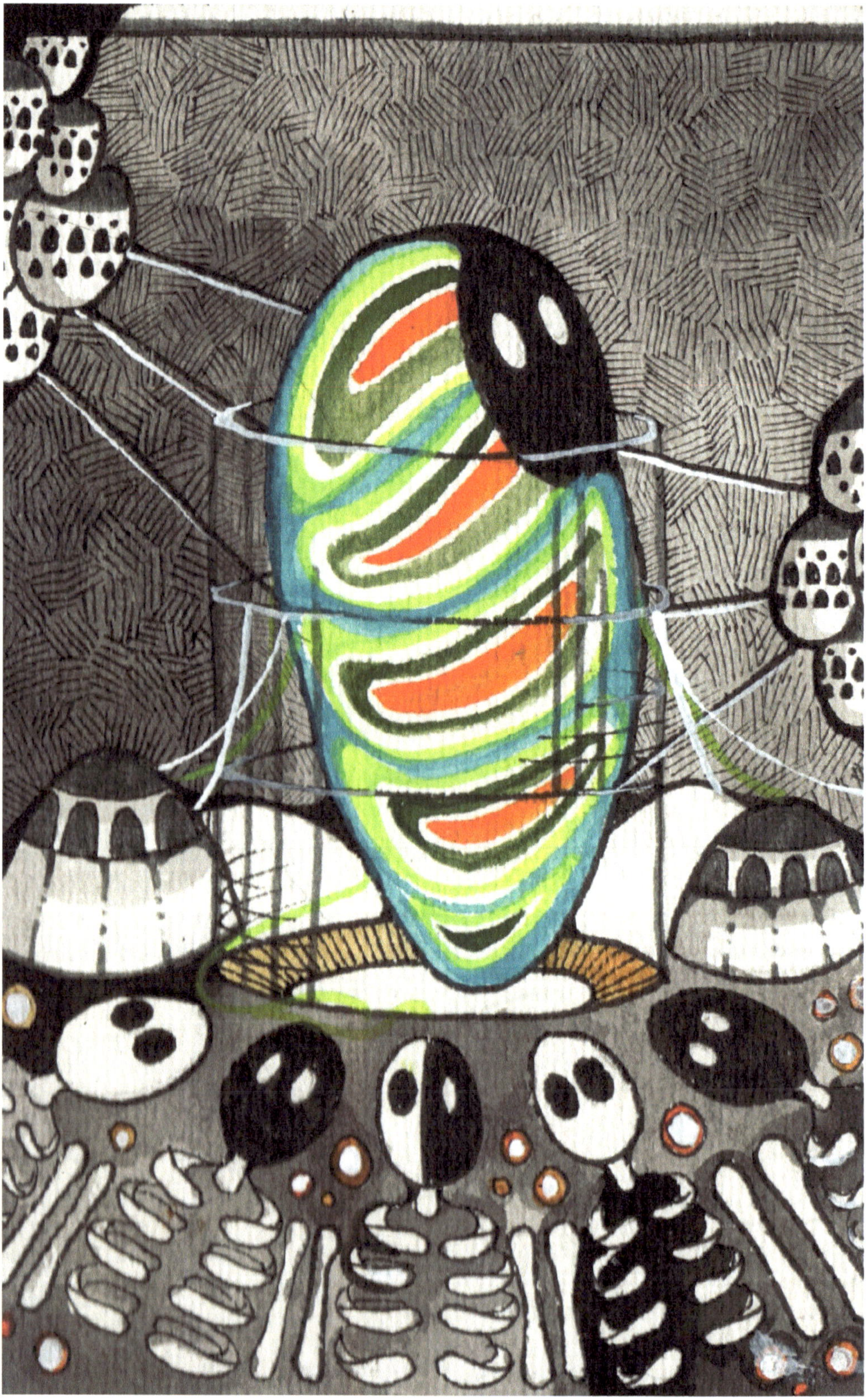

The Skeletons

OCT 2 6 2022

Something had to die for me to be here.
Something had to die for me to be here. I'm standing on the shoulders of my own fossils.
How can I ever call myself alone?
Everyone I've ever been... all thier spirits
they are the wind in my sails.

People are Fragile Kingdoms.
They are built upon layers and layers of themselves. The fossils of everyone I've ever been rest beneath me.

"Oh, this body is built on the ruins of
all the people who I've ever been
Wise men build their houses on rocks
(While the rest of us settle for skeletons)
The rest of us settle for skeletons.

-From "the Simplest Words" by The Narcissist Cookbook

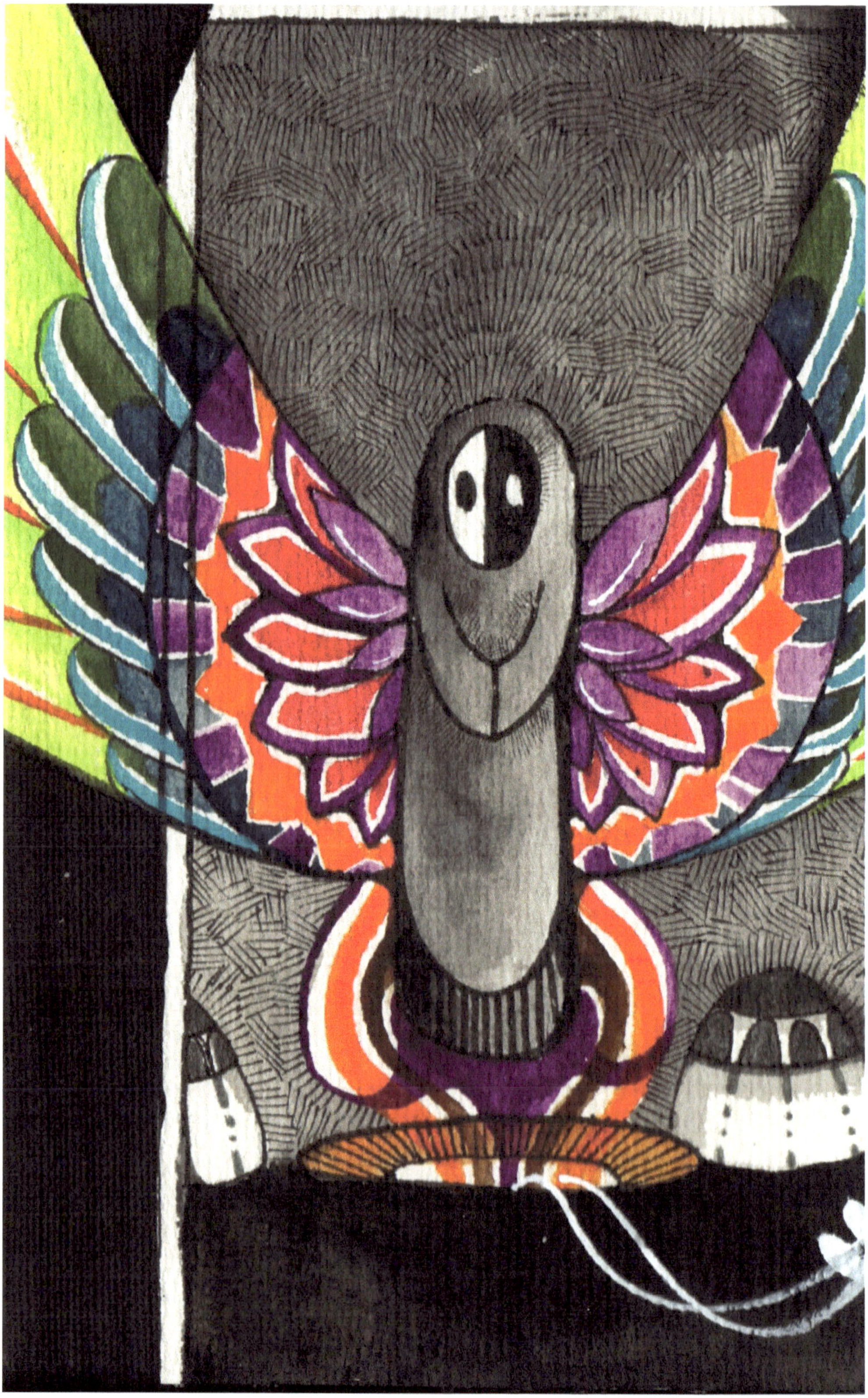

The Launchpad

OCT 27 2022

And here, at the launchpad, After all that
we've been through.
I confuss, I have'nt the slightest clue
where I'm going
what I should be doing.
But that's okay.
Don't birds sometime fly
just because they like the wind in thier feathers?

Citizens of the Patchwork House of Night always gather around the top floors when there is a Launch. The Whole House ripples as thoughts, actions and ideas move up in droves.

The Launch ends with the House getting bigger. Sometimes we have Launches every day. Other times it can be years between them.

One day, we will have our last launch and we will stay as that person, that version of the House until we collapse into the sea and into oblivion.

I wonder how tall we will be then.

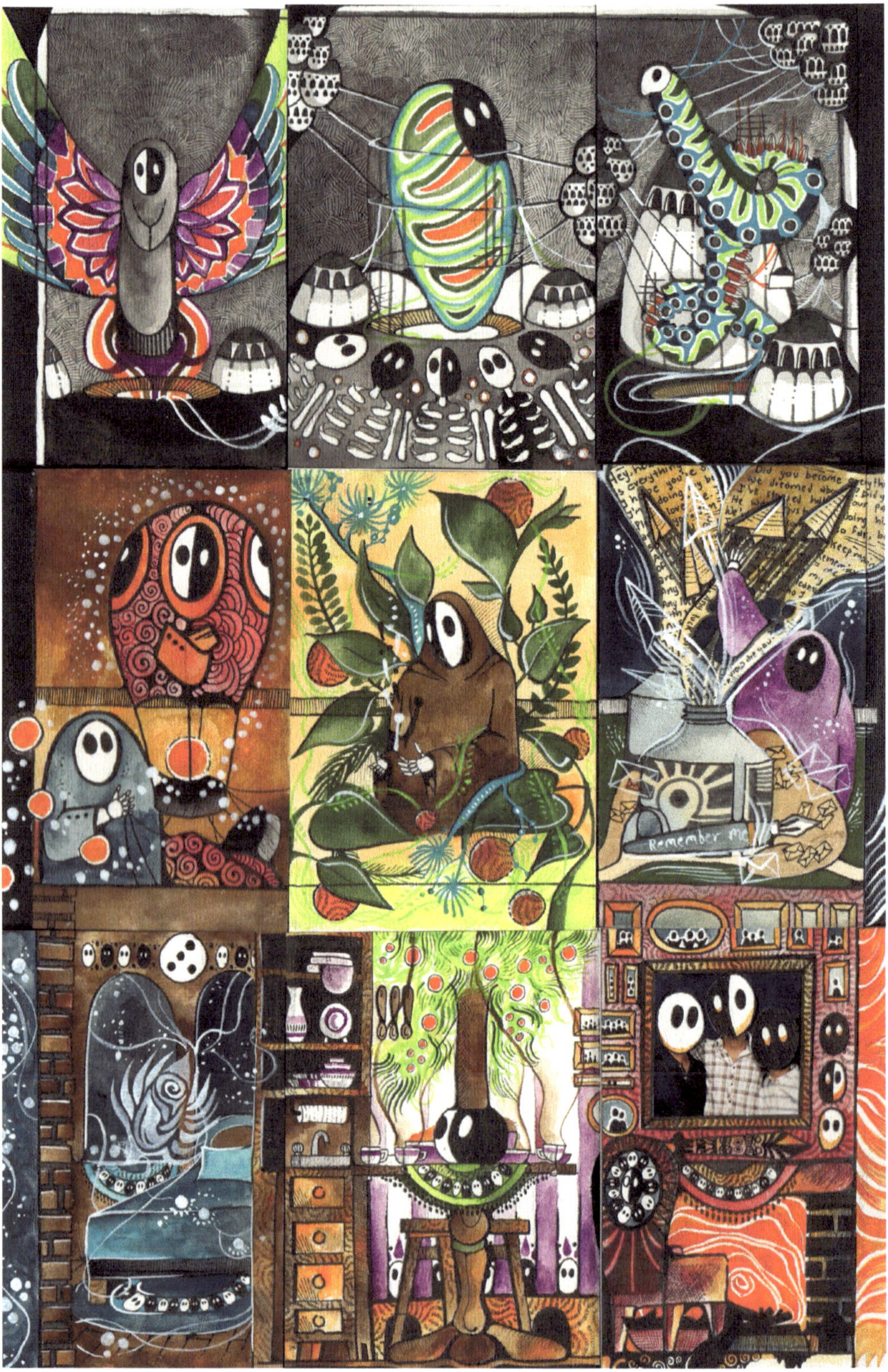
Remember me

THE FUTURE

Who made the world?
Who made the swan, and the black bear?
Who made the grasshopper?
This grasshopper, I mean—
the one who has flung herself out of the grass,
the one who is eating sugar out of my hand,
who is moving her jaws back and forth instead of up and down—
who is gazing around with her enormous and complicated eyes.
Now she lifts her pale forearms and thoroughly washes her face.
Now she snaps her wings open, and floats away.
I don't know exactly what a prayer is.
I do know how to pay attention, how to fall down
into the grass, how to kneel down in the grass,
how to be idle and blessed, how to stroll through the fields,
which is what I have been doing all day.
Tell me, what else should I have done?
Doesn't everything die at last, and too soon?
Tell me, what is it you plan to do
with your one wild and precious life?

-Mary Oliver

THE PATCH-WORK TEMPLE

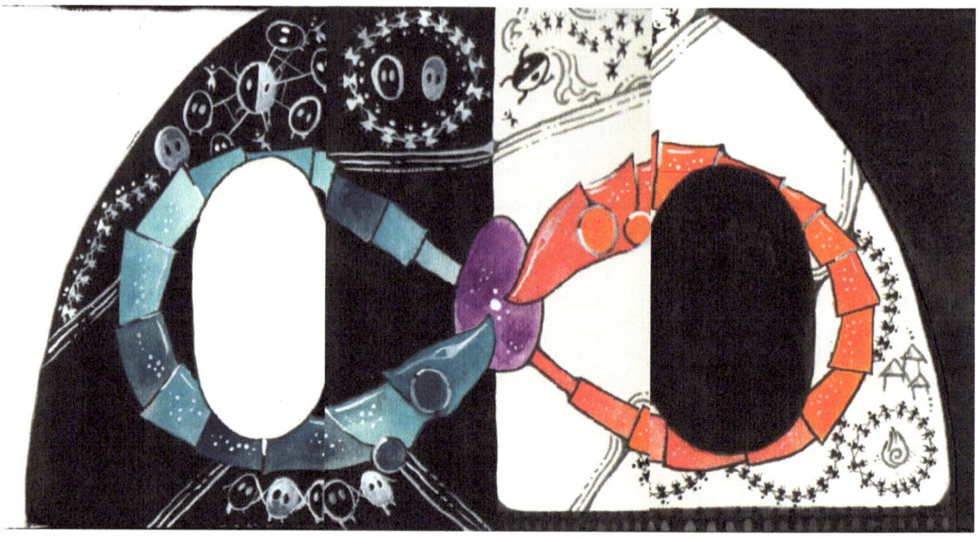

How did the Patchwork House of Night come to be? This is the question that is answered on the intricately carved walls of the Patchwork Temple. The runes tell a story of the Mindlands from eons ago. Thoughts coexisted and thrived, forming bustling communities and enriching their surroundings. However, they lived in fear of constant attack. Not from any outside force, but from the creator of the Mindlands himself. I would often lash out against my own mind, ravaging my mental landscape, eviscerating thoughts and purging ideas. Perhaps I hated myself and I needed everyone to know it.

The casualties were too high and so the thoughts came together and decided to take matters into their own cerebral hands.

Random thoughts, by no divine order and with no special pedigree, put on masks and came together to stand against me and my rampages. They were the first Patchwork People. And when they died, either in battle or of old age, they passed on their masks and mantle to a new generation of thoughts.

And over countless generations, they gradually built up the Patchwork House of Night, where new communities of Patchwork People put on the masks of their ancestors and join the cause. To protect me against myself until the end of my time.

THE SPIRE

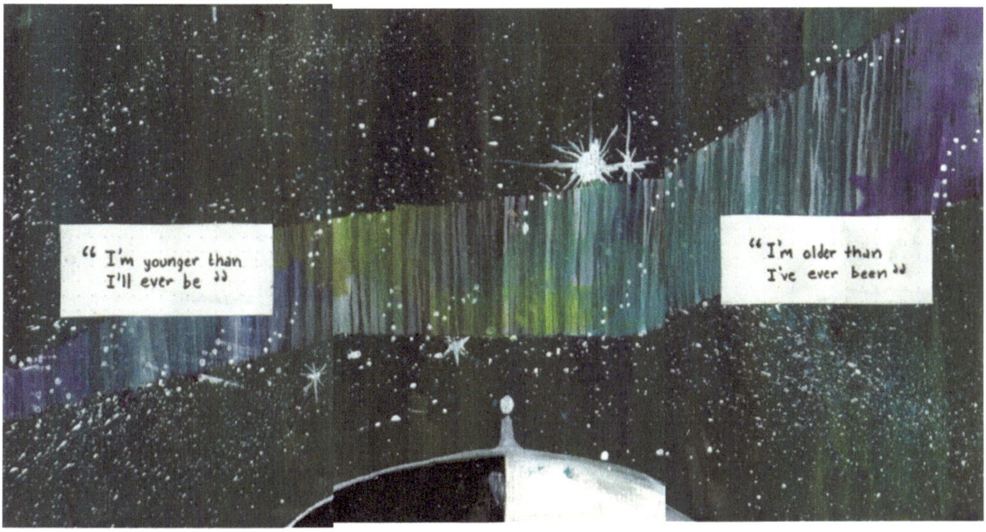

I wish I could bring my past selves up to the Spire with me. I wish they could see how far we've come. I would hold them close and tell them that I was greatful. They were doing their best. I intend to carry on their legacy.
And if you're reading this, who knows how many countless memories from now, I have some questions for you.
You know them by heart. We've asked them so many times before.
Hey, How are you? Are you well? Are you eating and sleeping okay?
Did we become everything we dreamed of? I'll do my best for you. I hope I've done enough.
I miss you and I haven't even become you yet.
Oh also....any luck with love?

"In three words I can sum up everything I've learned about life:

It goes on"

Robert Frost

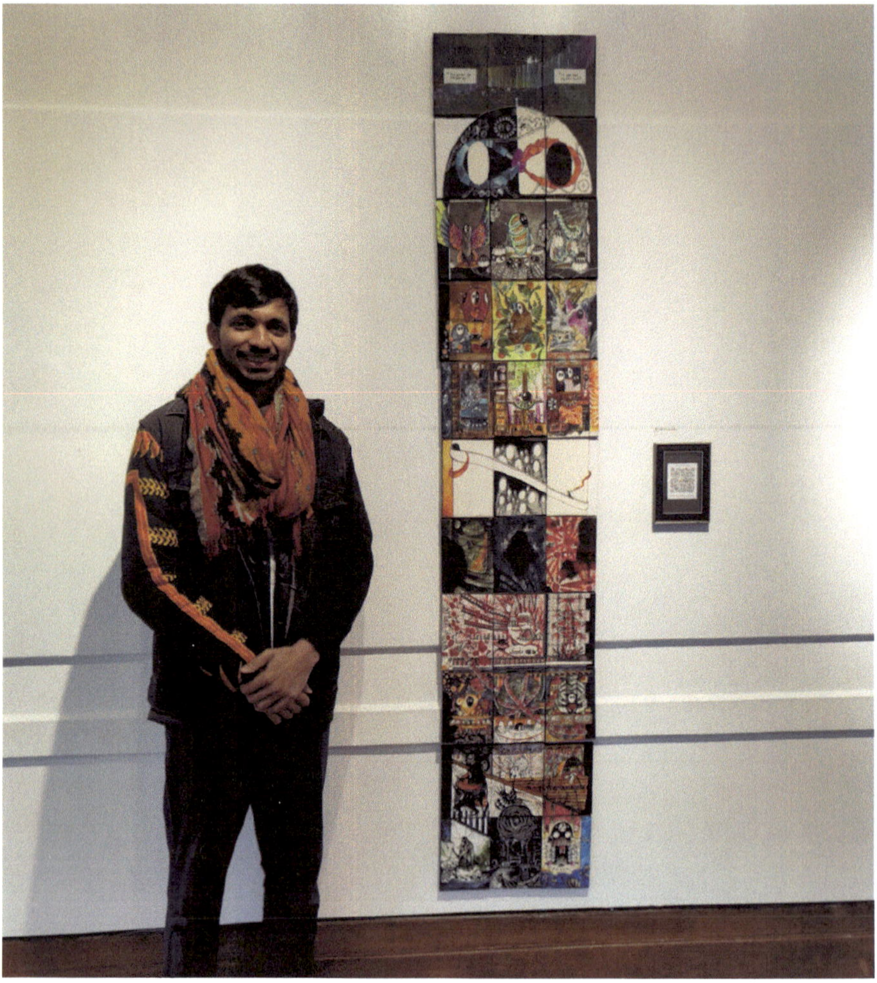

Ujwal Mantha is an interdisciplinary artist currently based in Toronto. His work prioritizes concepts over mediums and revolves around stories. He's also the one writing this bio and feels a bit pretentious for using the third person.
So I won't.
As I was saying, I like stories and I'm especially interested in how they can be used as ways to discuss identity, culture and imagination. I'm currently working on a large project, of which the Patchwork House is a small part: The Fragile Empires Project. What if people weren't individuals but entire communities unto themselves?
You can find more of my work on my website, the link for which you may find on the last page. I'd also encourage you to write to me should you have any stories of your own to share. I'm always ready to hear a good story.
Thank you for your time.

The Patchwork House of Night was a part of 37th Annual Juried Exhibition "Chrysalis" where it won the 2nd Prize in the Visual Arts Category.
It will continue to be exhibited in various places. The details of which you may find on my website.

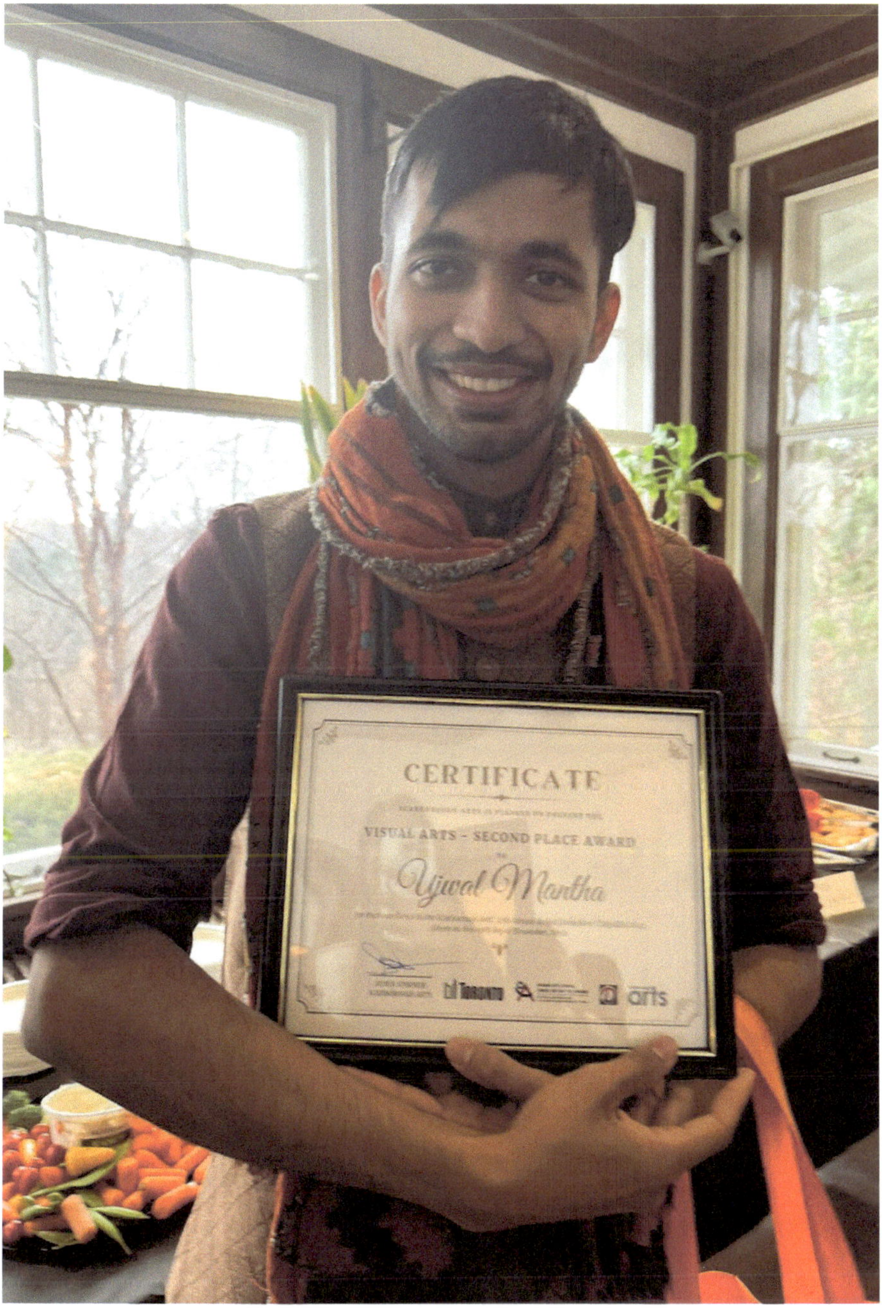

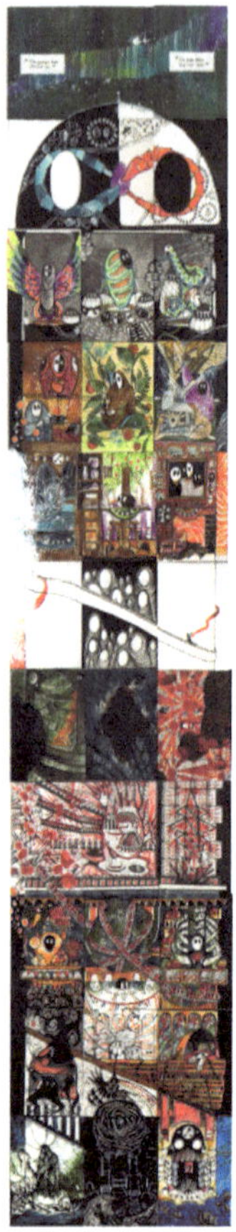

The Patchwork House of Night

UJWAL MANTHA

ujwalmantha.com
ujwalmantha@gmail.com